PRAISE

Angels on the Clothesline

"Tuzman's memoir is a treasure. Profoundly moving. The daughter of holocaust survivors transforms painful memory into a triumph of empathy, an epiphany of love. Her vignettes read like poetry, gems of sympathy, understanding, resistance. *Angels on the Clothesline* conjures a dream state of love for children and their wisdom. Can break the hardest heart wide open."

—RAFFI CAVOUKIAN, singer, author,
   founder of Raffi Foundation for Child Honouring

"*Angels on the Clothesline* is an exquisite invitation into self-compassion. Ani Tuzman brings us into the heart of the child she was, growing up in the shadow of the Holocaust. We see through the eyes of a girl whose spirit, despite the burden of trauma in her life, is not diminished, but shines ever more strongly. Ani's story inspires us to recognize the invincible light we each carry and to look for that light in each other. At this time on our planet when we need the healing power of love, *Angels on the Clothesline* is a stunning guide."

—MARCI SHIMOFF, #1 *New York Times* bestselling author
   of *Happy for No Reason* and *Love for No Reason*

"*Angels on the Clothesline* is a tender and intimate story of a young girl's search for belonging in the face of intergenerational trauma—and how she turns her wonder into a wellspring of love. With courage and imagination, Ani Tuzman gives us an irresistible invitation to see no stranger, starting with parts of ourselves we do not yet know."

—VALARIE KAUR, bestselling author of *See No Stranger*
   and founder of the Revolutionary Love Project

"The stories shared in Ani Tuzman's memoir intersect with many Black American families' generational trauma. This book is a cross-cultural experience to which many oppressed and marginalized groups will be able to relate. *Angels on the Clothesline* will be a great addition to curriculum with youth and young adults of color. I envision a study guide that could help unpack the effects of trauma from racism, othering, and bias, using storytelling as a way of exploring and healing trauma."

—**ANDREA KIRKSEY**, Executive Director of DOOR
(Discovering Opportunities for Outreach and Reflection) Chicago

"I love this book! It's a real, gritty, and tender delivery of a rich tapestry of experience through the eyes of an innocent child. In Ani's ability to share the child's light as well as wounds, we have a remarkable model of what it means for the gold within us to be brought forth through adversity. The detail brings these juicy stories alive, and the light and heart-beauty throughout is inspiring. What a gift."

—**JEANNIE ZANDI**, spiritual teacher, director of Living as Love

"This captivating story of survival and resilience is especially timely, given the rise in antisemitism and racist violence in our country. Ani Tuzman's memoir, *Angels on the Clothesline* deepens the understanding of the trauma wrought by antisemitism. I am inspired by the possibility of using *Angels on the Clothesline* for book groups and educational programs in churches and in interfaith groups throughout the country. An accompanying discussion guide will draw readers into reflection about universal questions of identity, racism and prejudice, suffering, hatred, survival, compassion, and healing. This memoir has truly universal reach."

—**REVEREND NANETTE SAWYER**, author of *Hospitality—The Sacred Art*

"A profoundly moving and eloquent story of how the Holocaust shaped lives of the children of refugee survivors. Tuzman, both poet and mystic, leads us into the life of a remarkably sensitive young girl as she bridges two worlds, two histories, and two beliefs about people—evil to the core or shining with an unquenchable inner light. I taught a college senior seminar on the Holocaust for many years, and I know the memoir literature quite well. *Angels on the Clothesline* is so compelling, so extraordinarily powerful, that I would without question assign it to my students. *Angels on the Clothesline* is literally unforgettable."

—PENNY GILL, Mary Lyon Professor of Humanities, emerita,
   Mount Holyoke College, author of *The Radiant Heart of the Cosmos*
   and *What in the World Is Going On?*

"From the soul of a child and imbued with the wisdom of a healer and teacher, Ani Tuzman's memoir is filled with tenderness and love. It is astounding how the simple language and the rhythm of her vignettes evoke such profound emotion. In her book, *Angels on the Clothesline,* Ani Tuzman chronicles human harm and trauma with beauty, poetry, and a depth of understanding that gently hold and heal that trauma."

—RABBI SHEILA WEINBERG, creator of the Jewish Mindfulness
   Teacher Training Program, poet, and author of *God Loves the Stranger*
   and *Let Us All Breathe Together*

"*Angels on the Clothesline* speaks to the heart and soul of all who have longed for belonging, acceptance, and unconditional love. In the face of pain, shame, and disappointment, Ani Tuzman was able to see the light in those she encountered and to find awe in the simple things around her. Her book opens the way for students to begin conversations about feeling marginalized, rejected, 'being the other,' and not being seen or heard. *Angels on the Clothesline* is both a resource to empower those who have lived through challenging experiences, and a profoundly insightful resource for educators and other professionals working with those who have faced adverse experiences. Ani Tuzman's story inspires us to cultivate our ability to see—and to teach others to see—the innate goodness in people. We are reminded that trauma does not define us."

—LOURDES ALVAREZ-ORTIZ, PhD, school psychologist,
   consultant, author of *Teaching to Strengths: Supporting Students
   Living with Trauma, Violence, and Chronic Stress*

"This book is for anyone who was a highly sensitive child—who has ever been different, been othered, been bullied, and who has fled the outside world to seek solace in their own imagination. Tuzman's writing is emotionally evocative, visually compelling, heartbreaking, and familiar."

—RICKI BLOOM, Licensed Clinical Social Worker,
   community organizer, social justice advocate

"Seeing, hearing, honoring: these are the underlying themes of Ani Tuzman's beautiful, heartbreaking, extraordinary memoir of childhood as a spiritually and psychologically sensitive, strong, intuitive, and imaginative daughter of two Holocaust survivors growing up in an environment in which she could not be seen, heard, or honored. *Angels on the Clothesline* is a deeply moving and important book that shares a tremendous amount of truth about being human, both in a very particular time and place, and far beyond."

—RABBI NANCY FLAM, cofounder of the National Center for Jewish
   Healing, founding director of the Institute for Jewish Spirituality

"Ani Tuzman's memoir sings with resilience. *Angels on the Clothesline* calls the reader to compassion for the small child within each of us, and to the love that can unite us all."

—MEIRA WARSHAUER, composer, *Living Breathing Earth Symphony*
   and *Ocean Calling*

"This book resonates in the deepest places. It will serve as a rich and important companion for anyone facing into difficult memories and beginning to uncover and connect with long-abandoned parts of themselves. *Angels on the Clothesline* is a courageous and generous work of compassionate art. Thank you, Ani Tuzman, for offering it to the world."

—NAN CAREY, teacher, therapist, poet

Angels on the Clothesline

Angels on the Clothesline

A MEMOIR

ANI TUZMAN

Published by Dancing Letters Press
60 Depot Road, Hatfield, MA 01038

Printed in the United States of America

Cover Design by Laura Duffy
Interior Design by Karen Minster

Publisher's Cataloging-in-Publication data
Tuzman, Ani, author.
Angels on the clothesline : a memoir / Ani Tuzman.
Hatfield, MA: Dancing Letters Press, 2023.
978-0-9974844-9-6 (hardcover) | 978-0-9974844-6-5 (paperback)
978-0-9974844-7-2 (ebook)| 978-0-9974844-8-9 (audiobook)
LCSH Tuzman, Ani. | Children of Holocaust survivors–United States–Biography.
Psychic trauma–Transmission. | Psychic trauma–Social aspects.
Psychic trauma–Biography. | Bullying. | Antisemitism. | Creative writing–Therapeutic use.
BISAC BIOGRAPHY & AUTOBIOGRAPHY / Personal Memoirs
BODY, MIND & SPIRIT / Inspiration & Personal Growth
SELF-HELP / Creativity | FAMILY & RELATIONSHIPS / Bullying
LCC D804.3 .T89 2023 | DDC 940.53/1809253—dc23

FIRST EDITION

Dancing Letters
PRESS

FOR THE CHILDREN

When who I really am sees who you really are,
all there is,
is love.

Morty Lefkoe

Contents

Welcome

Dear Reader,

A few words of welcome and context as you enter this book.

This was an unexpected memoir. I was deep into writing and researching a novel inspired by my parents' stories of surviving the Holocaust when, one morning on my way to my desk, I had a spontaneous vision of the young girl I was, crying in her bed. Responding to what felt like a summons, I sat down and wrote:

> I see you in your bedroom, lights out,
> your brother snoring in the next bed
> Nightly, he drifts away mid-whisper
> leaving you alone again.

I was at once the child in that bedroom and the woman witnessing my sadness. Thus began my journey and this memoir of bridging time to be the presence missing from my childhood. I recognized the imprint of trauma. I felt the painful weight of grief, bigotry, and fear. I also saw the innate wonder and light that I carried within, which no measure of darkness could extinguish.

Angels on the Clothesline is my story and also an invitation to embrace ourselves and each other with compassion. Because it is never too late to see and be seen with love.

With gratitude,
Ani

List of Vignettes

Angels on the Clothesline

You aren't very tall but just tall enough to see the newspaper open and flat
where your daddy left it on the shiny white kitchen table with the tiny
gold flakes. *Formica*, your mother calls it, proud of her modern
new table, her new English word.

You stare so hard at the long page your eyes water. All those marks
crowded together. Tall ones and skinny. Some with hats. Boots. Tails.
Big-bellied ones. Wiggly. Some would push others out of their way if
they could like they're in a hurry to get to the end of the page. To jump
off its edge. To rush out into the world.

Your daddy will be back. Will pick up his paper. Say things in Yiddish
to your sad mother standing at the sink, the stove. Her back to him.
Once in a while, she'll stop. Wipe her hands on her apron. Listen.
Or she'll scream suddenly, *Chas v'Chalila! Choleira! Such dogs!*
They should eat dirt! How mad she gets scares you.
No matter how often she hollers, you never get used to it.
Once in a blue moon your daddy laughs at what the marks say.
Even your mother, who hardly ever laughs, might laugh too.
Never for long though.

Some days, he looks down at the big crinkly pages for a long time.
Doesn't say a word, eyes moving from side to side under his thick
glasses, when all of a sudden, he pounds his fist on the table, making
your mother's shoulders lift up. And stay up. Stiff. Like someone
was sticking a gun in her back, only no one is. Not like what happened
to the grandparents you will never meet, the uncles and aunts
only children then. For some it was guns. In their backs or their fronts.
For your mother's favorite cousin, Rifka, and her crying baby,
a pitchfork. Most had to get naked first before the gas was pumped in.
There was no escape.

You want to know, ache to know, how those important black marks,
crawling, running, lined up like soldiers, like prisoners trapped inside
those pages, turn into things your daddy tells your mother. How can he
know their secrets just by looking at them? Sometimes, he takes off
his glasses. Holds the newspaper close to his face. As if to hear
the marks whisper their messages. And he does hear.
But no matter how long you stare after he leaves the kitchen.
No matter how close you get to those black marks
that squirm like squiggly bugs stuck in straight rows,
still their magic code stays secret from you.

Your mother can figure out the marks. Not as fast or easy as your daddy.
But she can *read*. That's what it's called you find out, this magic of
the marks coming to life and telling things. Like that the price for a
dozen eggs will drop so low soon chicken farmers like your daddy will
go out of business, which makes your mother put her head in her hands
and cry, and your father say he wasn't made to be a chicken farmer
anyhow. *Just wait. I'll show them.* Those times
you wish the newspaper was not even here. If you knew how
you would read the marks first, hide them from your parents
if the marks said bad things. Tell them the newspaper got lost.

You ask your daddy please will he help you learn to read. He says *No.*
When you go to school you can learn. And it won't be
the Yiddish newspaper. You'll learn to read in Anglish.
He says it like it doesn't matter how long it will take. He doesn't
understand that you can't wait, that you don't care if the marks
are Yiddish or American. You just want to know them.

So you stare and stare and stare, until you start to see
the same ones hiding in different places in those long pages.
You pretend the marks are happy you are finding them, that they
want you to know them so that one day, all of a sudden,

what was secret will not be secret anymore.

While you wait for them to talk to you like they do to your daddy,
you talk to the marks. Quietly inside your mind. Ask them to please
say things that will make your parents happy instead of so sad, so mad,
so afraid the Nazis will come to America too.

Writing is making your own marks, your daddy says one day
After that it's even harder to wait. You have to be as patient
as the willow who never gets mad. You decide that when you
can finally write, you will write marks that take away
your parents' sadness. Maybe other people's sadness too.
You will write things not in their newspaper. Good
things that maybe will make them happy they are alive.
Even if none of the people they love still are.

You keep practicing.
Wonder if *this* time they will believe
you really did die. Face down in the cold water.
Not moving.
Not any single little part of you.
Like a real dead girl floating.

They probably aren't even watching
from where they sit up the sand hill with the other
greena—what they call themselves, short for greenhorns—
in their circle of fold-open beach chairs
crooked from sinking into the sand. But they don't mind,
happy to be together. Talking fast. Telling Yiddish
jokes. Your mother laughing so hard she can't
stop coughing on her lawn chair. Crisscross of yellow holding her up.
A baby in her belly big as a watermelon.

After pretending to be dead long as you can, you have to stop
even though you never want to. You stand.
Dig your toes into the soft bottom, the water so clear
you watch your toes bury themselves like fleshy worms
the river rushes over on its way into woods you are
not allowed to swim into.

You see Sigmund, who married Rita after her first husband died,
hand your daddy a can of Schlitz beer. You took a sip once
but spit it out right away, making your daddy laugh and say
What does a child know. More cans get pulled from the orange coolers
they bring to the beach to keep things cold, with sandwiches in them
and best of all watermelons they cut into slices that hardly ever run out,
full of seeds for spitting wars with your brother that

your parents let you have when they're in a good mood.
Which they almost always are at A Lion's Beach.

No matter how hot it gets, none of the *greena* go into the water, except
for Franya Hertz. And your daddy. Who any minute might give his
glasses to your mother, run down the hill and dive in. A belly dive
because it's not very deep. Except for the part
with the slimy green underwater arms that grab. And the quicksand
that soon as it feels your toe in it will suck you in like
that cowboy you watched on television who screamed the whole time
until his mouth went under too.

Sometimes your daddy stays in, flips you backwards off his shoulders.
Like he's having a good time too, like he's forgetting
all the terrible things.
Your mother never comes in. Except on the very hottest days.
Just her toes at the very edge.
But you don't mind being alone because
you're not. Sparkles of sunlight are everywhere you look.
They play on the shiny water. And when the wind tickles the river
to give it goosebumps, you get goosebumps too. The good kind.

You put your head back in, stretch out your arms in front,
your legs straight behind. Like you are an arrow.
You stop hearing their voices. How the whole world goes quiet
is your favorite part of the dead girl's float.
How you can make everything disappear.

You stand. Turn to face where the river first rushes from the dark woods.
A place you're scared to swim. So far from the sandy shore.
So deep your feet can't reach the bottom.
You swim toward it now. The river pushes you back.
You swim harder. Feel your strongness. Dare
let one leg drop to check for the green stuff

even stringier and slimier than spinach.
It's there. You swim away fast as you can,
the river helping you get back to where you
can see the bottom. And your feet.

Any minute your mother will come down the hill and holler
Your lips are blue. It's time to come out. Like always you will
pretend not to hear her, quick do the dead girl's float.
A super long one.
She'll still be there when you come up. Yelling *It's time now!*
Once in a blue moon your daddy comes to get you out.
But after maybe two shouts he smiles and gives up
like he understands why you love swimming and never
want to come out. You hope no one
will come for a long time today. Turning blue
doesn't bother you.

When someone calls your name, it's not your mother's voice.
It's Franya Hertz. Calling you in a kind way.
With a blue towel not from your house spread wide in her hands
like it was hanging on a clothesline.
You look past her up the hill. See your mother's chair gone.
Your father's too. Franya comes closer, water
covering her ankles now. She says in Yiddish not to be afraid.
Then in English, *The baby is coming.*
Franya tells you your daddy took your mommy to the hospital.
A place where they will take good care of her. And the new baby.
Franya will take care of you, she says close to your ear,
and also of your little brother Marty, who you see digging with a spoon
near where your mother's chair was,
dumping spoonful after spoonful of sand on his head.

Even after you're not cold inside the blue towel
Franya wraps around you, you can't stop shivering.

You figured out the scream you heard from under the water
was your mother screaming. You're afraid
because of how afraid she sounded. You don't
tell this to Franya who surprises you, in a good way, when she
picks you up and, slow, carries you up the hill, then sits down.
Quiet. You on her lap. Her arms around the towel that's around you.
You feel the crookedness under both of you. The way her chair
is not straight in the hot sand. But you don't care.
Because even if her chair tips all the way over, she
won't let go, you are pretty sure, happy
to be in the cave Franya's arms make, until
you'll be alone again.

Before your mother comes back from the hospital,
Nurse comes. Tall as the Jolly Green Giant. But Nurse
wears white. Her shoes. Her socks. Her skirt. Her blouse. Her sweater.
And the funny little hat high up on top of her head
that reminds you of an upside-down
coleslaw box.

Nurse tells Marty and you, standing very still in front of her,
Your main job is don't be big burdens for your mother.
And stay out from under Nurse's feet.

When it's time for bed, she picks you and Marty up like two bugs
or maybe two pieces of dust and she is a gigantic
vacuum cleaner. She puts your brother under one arm.
You under the other, kicking. But not too hard.
Because you are afraid of Nurse.
You don't tell her when her coleslaw-box hat
tips like a candle getting crooked on top of a birthday cake.

Nurse *never* smiles.
You decide it must be against the rules.
Just like making too much noise and
bothering your mother when she finally comes home
with the new baby. A sister.
Who you aren't supposed to bother either.
Wrapped in blankets not wrapping paper.
A gift for your mother. Not for you.

You hear your daddy tell his brother, Uncle Maier,
it cost a lot of money he didn't have for Nurse to come to the farm
But a wife you take care of, he says.

He doesn't want Esther to hurt her back again like she did
after Marty was born in Brooklyn and she had to carry him
and groceries and you and Marty's carriage up five flights of stairs
while your daddy sewed buttonholes in the Bronx.

You don't care why he decided to buy Nurse.
You hate her. And the new baby, too, who
made this all happen and who your mother keeps
close to her like she will break if anyone but her or Nurse
picks her up. You kind of wish she would break. But not really.
If she just wasn't here anymore that would be enough.
Maybe the hospital can take her back,
gets you a spanking when you say it. So you never say it again.
Not one of all the times you keep wishing it.

The baby sister becomes their favorite. Not like you who
doesn't want to eat the spinach and the peas on her plate,
or come in from playing outside when it gets dark,
or get mercurochrome
on her cuts or have a sister.

The letters have been there this whole time. High up.
Watching and waiting from over the blackboard. Silent.
You've been watching too. And waiting. These
aren't crowded into your daddy's Yiddish newspaper.
These belong to English.

Tall ones stand beside short ones like mother letters
keeping their babies close. They never make any noise.
You wish they would. Maybe they get loud at night
when no one is in the kindergarten class in the cellar
where the cubbies are and three toilets for girls.
Maybe then, all alone in the cellar, the letters come to life.
Start to march in their high places. One behind the other
circling the classroom. You picture them playing leapfrog,
shouting their names and the sounds they make to the desks below,
to the empty chairs. Bowing as they do. Climbing down
to dance on the desks. Laughing.
Making lots of noise.

It's so hard to wait.
You ask again. Your belly full of butterflies.
When will the teacher teach everyone to read?
She tells you *It's not time yet, Ann,*
to be introduced to the letters.
You don't like her saying your name wrong,
but worse is when she says, *You must wait patiently.*

You can tell she forgot what it's like
to be someone who doesn't know how to read yet.
She also forgot that learning to read
is the most important thing in kindergarten. More important

than making pictures of holidays your family
doesn't even know the names of or celebrate.
Like when she makes the class paste paper feathers
on a paper turkey, all the turkeys exactly the same,
though you are not even a little bit like the other children
and your holidays aren't either.
You don't mind pasting cotton balls to a cut-out Christmas tree
because you like snow. Of course, you crinkle up the green paper tree
and its cotton-ball snow and throw it in the garbage as soon as
get home. So your mother won't cry and your daddy curse
about America turning their children into *goyim*. Strangers.
Ashamed to be Jews.

This whole time you've been sneaking peeks
at the out-of-reach quiet letters. Especially the letter *A*
the first letter of your name that makes an *Eh* sound
when your parents say it but a different sound
when Americans like the kindergarten teacher call you.

At breakfast your brother asks why you keep staring
at the back of the cereal box. *I am finding A's*
you tell him but he doesn't care one bit. Thinks it's
stupid. Says cereal is for eating, not for looking hard at
the back of its box. He doesn't understand
that when you can finally read, you will be able to open
so many secret boxes. Too many
to even count. And without a grown-up.

Reading will be a dream come true.
The biggest dream of all.
Except maybe for writing. Writing is a miracle
too big to even imagine.

Dr. Falheimer comes to the farm driving
his red sports car that can barely fit his belly
and his black fat doctor bag full of gaggers
and needles. You don't pee on his pointy shoes
on purpose. You're as surprised as he is.

He doesn't show how much he really doesn't
like your pee on his shiny shoes, black socks,
the bottoms of his shiny black pants—wet now
and getting a little smelly. Your parents say
We are so sorry, a bunch of times.
They tell you to say so. You do, but don't
really mean it. You're even a tiny bit glad
the pee came out but don't dare say that.
All those times he hurt you and your brother.
Made you bend over his big knee with your
panties pulled down so he could stick in
his sharp stinging needle.
He never said he was sorry.

When you say you won't let Dr. Falheimer
give you a needle without Kathy there,
they all get even madder. No one knows
where Kathy is. They promise they will
help you find her later. You scream *No!*
Make yourself strong as you can. Keep
yelling *No.* Wiggle a ton. Kick the air when
Dr. Falheimer asks you to be calm.
Hands in tight fists, you hold your shorts
up. Don't let him force them down.

Dr. Falheimer, his wet socks and his
wet shoes dried with a *shmata* by your mother,
tries to act patient. Says, *Let the little girl find
her doll.* Waits with his hands resting on his
belly like it was a soft round shelf made for
putting arms and hands on, while your mother
looks for Kathy and you pretend to.

They think you know just where Kathy is,
that you hid her before the doctor knocked.
The truth is Kathy hid herself. She doesn't
want Dr. Falheimer to touch her either.

Without moving your lips or making a sound,
you whisper to Kathy that she's a doll and
dolls don't get shots in their tooshies. She
doesn't have to be scared. Can let you find her.
So she does. Behind the couch.
You hug her tight. Feel her hug you back,
your eyes full of tears because
everyone is so mad at you and because
a needle is coming. You go stand
in front of Dr. Falheimer who is
holding his needle. A mean gleam in his eyes
like he's happy to stab you after what you did to him.

In your mind you tell Kathy not to be afraid.
Soon it will be over. She won't feel anything,
only you will. You know she'll stay close and
she won't be mad no matter what. Not if you cry.
Don't act like a big girl. Are not at all
brave like your parents were in The War.
Kathy will love you just the same as always.
She never takes her love away.

Your parents say, *Thank you very, very much*
to Dr. Falheimer for his visit. But you don't.
He puts his doctor bag into his red car.
Squeezes himself in. Puts the top down.
Waves goodbye. You don't wave back.

After he's gone for sure, you take Kathy
way out past the coops. Far as you can get
from the kitchen where your father
keeps saying, *It's a shanda, a disgrace.* You
making such a big gevalt
over a little needle.

BLOUSE

So little you are. Still new to kindergarten and
to setting out your school clothes the night before.
A wire hanger hung on the doorknob.
Looped over its hook, your panties and white *hemdella*,
Undershirt it's called in English.
You pick your favorite blouse, white
with a ruffle of pink lace around its collar,
to wear with your red corduroy jumper.
You are happy with your choice.
You don't have too many.

In the morning, your mother doesn't like
the blouse you picked and are buttoning up.
She says, *Take it off right now.*

But this is the one I want to wear.
I want to wear THIS one. The words just bust out of you.
First time you ever go against your mother, afraid
of what will happen next.

You little rotzer, she yells.
Yiddish for a little runny-nose girl who
doesn't know anything.
Because you were born in America,
you think you are so smart?

She is a storm growing in front of you.

Who are you to talk back to me!
A five-year-old rotzer with the chutzpah to tell her mother
what she *wants?* You taste the bitter in her words.

Her angriness bigger than the whole house.
She pulls the blouse off you. Throws it on the floor.
Then the worst part. She steps on it with her shoe,
twists her foot around like your blouse was
nothing but a *shmata*. A rag to wipe a dirty floor with.
Part of its pink lace tears off. Your best blouse.

When you bend to pick up a piece of ruffle,
she pulls you back.
You will learn a lesson, she yells so loud,
the roof might lift off from her screaming.
A mother and a father you honor like it says
in the Ten Commandments. If my mother—
she should only rest in peace—was still alive,
I would be kissing her feet.

She is shaking now. Her cheeks red like borscht
while she keeps screaming the lessons
you're supposed to learn.
You don't even try to bend down again.
But you will not learn the lessons.

You don't like your mother. A huge sin
against the Ten Commandments.
But you can't help it. Don't want to help it.
She took away your best blouse.
You won't let her take away
being mad at her.

Sweaty hot in your red snowsuit on the yellow school bus,
you feel a lump by your knee. Too hard to reach.
Deep inside your snow pants. Probably a bunched-up sock
your brother stuck in there at home, right before
you put on your snow pants.

In the kindergarten cellar by the cubbies, you start to
peel down your snowsuit. But change your mind
because what if he stuck panties in there not a sock.
Quick you switch your snow boots for school shoes.
Go to Girls Toilet #3. Shut the wood door.
Put the hook in its hole. Peel the pants part way down.

Your dress drops open like it's happy to be free.
The lump inside your tights still there. Warm
against your leg. You get a not-so-good
feeling in your belly.
Hold the bottom of your dress up and pull the tights down slow.
When you get to your knee, you see
a tail. You know before you see the rest.

A mouse.

Right next to your leg. Still warm.
It died there. In your tights.
A dead mouse *touching your leg this whole time.*
You feel like throwing up. But you can't now.
You can't throw up. Or let the tears come out.
You have to hide the dead mouse.

You take a deep breath.
Then just as quiet as a dead mouse, yank

its tail. Drop it in the little toilet.
Flush.
You watch it spin around not sure
a mouse can flush down a toilet.
You keep on keeping the tears back.

It goes down.
You watch for it to come back up, to slide up through the hole.
No one probably ever flushed a mouse down a toilet.
When it doesn't come back, you wait for the little toilet to break.
Then they will know what you did. That you tried
to hide a mouse that died inside your tights.

Most of all they will know they are right.
And now you know too that they are right when they
say Jews are filthy. That Jews stink. Who else
would have a still-warm dead mouse
inside her tights?

You're surprised when the teacher knocks on the wood door.
Asks if you are alright. You say you have a bad bellyache.
That's why you're taking so long. When your bellyache
feels better, you'll hang up your snow pants and
come to the kindergarten room. *Pretty soon,* you say,
so she won't wait. So she'll leave.
Fine then, she says back. *I hope to see you at your desk soon.*

You wonder if when you walk through the kindergarten door,
she will smell the mouse. What if,
even though you flushed it down it comes back up later?
When it does everyone will know
how a dead mouse got into the kindergarten cellar.
It was the little Jew who brought it.
Proof of how different you are. How stinky Jews are.
And how they can't hide it.

The first grade teacher shares her big announcement.
Children, tomorrow you will meet the letters.

The rest of the day you can't think about anything else.
Don't eat most of supper. Leftover chicken soup.
Boring carrots. Wrinkly peas.
You put your pajamas on early without anyone saying you should.
Get into bed. Squeeze your eyes shut tight
so sleep will come fast and morning be soon.

But what happens instead is
you see the letters. Shining in the dark behind your eyes
like the letters were made of light.
You tell the letters, without making a sound,
how happy you feel to be finally meeting them,
how much better life will be with reading.
But they must know that already.

At school, the letters are still high over the blackboard.
Out of reach.
You wonder when the teacher will bring them down.

But she doesn't.
Instead she writes *A* on the blackboard. The mama *A* and the baby *a*.
Then she makes their sound. So many times. Too many.
You are in a hurry to meet another letter you don't already know.
She introduces the letter *B*. Makes its sound.
Then she writes *B* with two *AA*s next to it. *BAA.*
She says *BAA BAA BAA.* Asks the class to copy her.
Everybody say BAA BAA BAA.
Pretty soon the room sounds like it's full of sheep.

You are too excited to keep *BAA*ing. Because now
you know how it works. Every letter has its own sound
and when you put them next to each other,
they make something new together.

Letters make words, the teacher tells everyone,
which you just figured out and makes you
want to jump up and down. But most of all
you just want her to keep going.
You would stay in your chair without going home for a week,
just so you could meet every letter in the Alphabet.

Then something wonderful happens.
The teacher says she has books
with all the letters in them and a lot of words they make.
She walks slowly down the rows. Puts a book on every desk.
You hug yours close. Getting this book is
the best thing that could happen to a person.

With nothing left in her hands, the teacher tells the class
not to look ahead in their books.
*So you won't get confused, we will meet the letters
one or two at a time.* I won't get confused,
you want to say right away.

Do you understand, my big first graders?
You nod your head like the rest of the class.
But you won't go slow. You just can't wait any more.
Maybe you'll just pretend to go slow. Act like it was enough to meet
big *A* and *B* with little *a* and *b* and say a bunch of *BAA*s.

All of a sudden you get scared the teacher will say
her big first graders must leave their books in their desks.
So she can be sure no one will turn more pages at home. But

she doesn't say it. The bell rings. Maybe she meant to say it
but forgot. You don't dare ask if it's okay
to bring the Alphabet home. You have been waiting
to meet these letters for so long. All your life.

The Ark is so new, you can smell its wood.
One of the fathers built it for Hebrew Sunday School.
Today is the first time you all climb the tall ladder
to the very top.

You look down. Pretend the blue carpet is water
just starting to get higher. You close your eyes. Listen
to the pounding rains. Just like in the story of Noah.
Rain that will not stop, that will cover everything.
But up here, you are safe.

The teacher is going to read a story. She waits
for all of you to sit down on the eight pillows
placed in the shape of a banana on the top of the Ark.
The whole time you hear the rain falling hard.

She reads about when God speaks to the Jewish people,
angry at them for doing something wrong. For kind of
forgetting he is God. *Are you ready?* she asks.
I have a special surprise for everyone.
She turns the book around and holds it up.

The ceiling light is so bright, you can't see
what's on the book's shiny page. You hear her say *This
is a picture of God.* She brings the book closer.
So everybody can have a good look.
You see a man with a white beard, so long it touches his big toes
that stick out of his sandals. He has kind eyes and a kind smile,
holds a crooked tree branch without any leaves
that the teacher calls his *staff.*

It's not true! busts out of your mouth without you even
raising your hand. *You can't have a picture of God.*
You start to cry, your lips like jello. Your legs, too, when you stand up.
You're not right! you say really loud,
sad and angry all mixed up inside you and spilling out.
Tears don't let you see the picture anymore,
like The Flood is in your eyes.

The teacher asks you to say you're sorry.
But you don't. Because you're not.
Her voice is by your ear now, saying you will have to
leave the Ark if you do not apologize.
You don't want to leave. The Flood will drown you.
But your mother says not to say you're sorry unless
you really mean it. You press your lips together
to not let *I'm sorry* come out.

You must leave the Ark right now, Ann, the teacher says.
She reaches for your hand. You let her hold it
because you have to.
She leads you to the top of the tall ladder. Tells you
to follow her down. You watch her put the front
of her high heel shoe on the first flat ladder step
then keep on going. You so much don't want to,
but you follow her, smell her perfume come down the ladder too.

At the bottom when you don't have to hold on anymore,
you wipe your runny nose with your sleeve.
The teacher points to the time-out chair.
Tells you to sit there and wait for your mother
to pick you up early because you are too *upset*
to stay in Hebrew school with the other children.
You wonder if *upset* means angry she told a lie.
But God is invisible. There can't be a picture of God.

You hear the teacher dial the phone and tell your mother
to come get you. Then she climbs back up the ladder.
Away from The Flood.

You can't make the crying stop. But not only that.
The water is getting higher. Almost up to your ankles.
Pretty soon it will reach your knees. You want to tell the teacher
The Flood is getting higher in case she didn't notice. Before long
it will cover the puzzles, the crayons, the books,
the chairs, and tables. It's already starting to cover the shoes
that everybody except the teacher took off before climbing
to the top of the Ark. The lunchboxes they left by their shoes will
probably float away with their coats.

If you holler up and tell the teacher, she might say
you are just imagining The Flood. So you don't.

You look around. If you and everything else floats away—
even the teacher's pocketbook and the time-out chair
and there is nothing left but water—
still, the teacher and the rest of the children
will be safe. Like Noah was and his family and all
the animals two-by-two Noah brought to the Ark.

Just in time your mother opens the door, letting
some of the water hurry out. She's wearing her brown coat.
A big surprise is that she doesn't look mad at you.
There are wrinkles in her forehead, more worried
than mad. She kneels down and opens her arms,
a different mother, not your regular one.

You don't wait for the teacher to say it's okay
to get off the time-out chair. You just run to your mother

right through The Flood. She lifts you up, so you don't
feel the water anymore. You get snot mixed with salty tears
all over her shoulder. But she doesn't make you move. She just
keeps hugging you. *Let's go honey*, she whispers into your wet hair,
maybe from tears, maybe from the heavy rain,
you can't tell which.

She puts you down. You get your soggy coat from its hook.
Your wet shoes and mittens. Put everything on. Take her hand.
She doesn't complain about how wet your mitten is in her dry glove.
The teacher calls down from up high, *Thank you Mrs. Tuzman.*
I hope Ann feels better and we will see her next Sunday.
Your mother doesn't say anything back, just squeezes your hand.
Next Sunday, you don't say out loud,
the Hebrew School will be all gone,
covered by water so deep, no one will be able to find it.

On the ride home your mother keeps being quieter
than her regular self. A long way down the road
she asks what happened in Sunday school.
You tell her about the picture of God.
She stays quiet a bunch more minutes, then finally says,
Nobody can see God with their eyes, my ketsella,
If only it were so easy.

Your mother lost her
sense of smell in The War.
She doesn't know when or where,
just that it's gone and never came back.
But once,
peeling an orange at the sink,
suddenly she calls out,
Gotenyu!
Holds the orange up as if the sun
had dropped, cool, into her hand.
It smells like a million tiny stars exploding.
She brings it close to her nose, breathes in deep,
tears rolling down her cheeks.
Like a million tiny stars, she whispers.
You think you hear her
thank her mother
for the miracle.

Even though you were there, you don't remember
your parents sleeping on Tanta Rae's floor for months
after they got off the boat in America.
No room for a crib in Tanta Rae and Uncle Menasha's
two-and-half-room apartment in the Bronx with
the peephole in the door,
their bedroom not much bigger than their bed.

Visits to the Bronx from the farm are only once in a while.
The worst part is going through the too-long tunnel with
walls like a huge bathroom you can't wait to get out of into the sunshine.
Even closing your eyes doesn't help. You still hear and feel being in it.

Finally, you're there. Everything always the same in 3A
on the third floor of the tall brick building with wide stairs and
hallways that echo. Tanta Rae on a step stool looking from inside
through the peephole to make sure it's safe to open up even though
she heard your daddy yell to her from the intercom downstairs.
It's us Rae. Arnold and Esther and the children.

The heavy door opens. *Let me look on you,* she says to you first,
the oldest. Then one at a time to everybody else.
Tanta Rae. The shortest grown-up you know.
Smiling big with her buck teeth. Her eyes
behind her big glasses bulging like a bug's. Like she has four eyes.
Her bad breath she's breathing all over everyone. But you don't mind.
It's just how Tanta Rae smells.
Okay, okay, Rae. Menasha, behind her with his hoarse voice.
Let them come in already. They are in a car such a long time.

The green glass candy dish always with the same candies.
The snake plant with leaves like knives that
Tanta Rae keeps on the fire escape so *the poor thing*
can get some light.
Tanta Rae in her apron at the sink in her tiny kitchen.
Tanta Rae on her tiptoes reaching for something.

Uncle Menasha tries to sneak you candies,
reaches out the green dish when Rae and your parents
aren't looking. You're not supposed to but want to take one
just because Uncle Menasha is offering.
He puts the green dish back on the lamp table
next to the fancy dancing woman with a blue lace
porcelain petticoat, Tanta Rae calls it, whose partner
has a white ponytail wig and gold buckles on his shoes.
So careful you all have to be around their dance, not to
bump or God forbid break them even by accident.
Most of the time quiet Uncle Menasha
just reads his Yiddish newspaper, peeking once in a while
over the top his spectacles with twinkly eyes
at *you.*

Kinndalach, they call your parents,
having no children themselves.
Tanta Rae, her accent so New York,
never talks about her sister.
The sister who was your father's mother and
who your middle name comes from.

Tanta Rae calls you *Channahla,* your mother's mother's name.
Asks if you want another sour pickle.
Reminds you often of how when your parents
first came to America with you inside your mother's belly,

they had nowhere to go,
how she and Menasha took them in. *Two orphans.*
We unrolled for them every night a mattress on the living room floor.
Uncle Menasha tried to get your father a job.
In the same factory where he worked.
But for your father a job in a factory
wasn't good enough. He had
too much ambition.

You never tell Tanta Rae your daddy thinks Menasha
doesn't have enough *ambition*, which you find out means
wanting to be better. To get ahead in this world.
Your daddy says he will never understand how someone
can live in America and never learn to read English.
How Menasha in *dem goldenna lahnd*
can be happy working in a factory his whole life.
What you don't understand most is how your Tanta Rae
cannot *read any language.* Not Yiddish or English.

Two at a time, because that's all that fits at her kitchen table,
everybody eats the whitefish your daddy paid for
on fresh sliced pumpernickel. Kielbasa on the table too.
Such a spread, Tanta Rae says. *You kinndalach must be doing okay.*

You think about her dead sister
who didn't leave Poland between the wars
like Tanta Rae did.

You paste paper feathers on a construction-paper turkey,
hoping it is not a sin, but how can you not do
what the teacher says. *Gobble gobble gobble*
spreads in the schoolroom like the swell of syllables
in the small Elmer synagogue when a cluster of
devout men dressed in black rock back and forth,
praising God. The second graders are not praising
the turkeys, you are pretty sure.

They seem to be having fun, which makes you think
this holiday is nothing like Passover or Yom Kippur.
Not sad. Not a time to remember being slaves in Egypt
or trying not to get sealed in a heavy Book of Life,
wondering *Who shall Die by Fire and Who by Stoning.*
Who by Drowning and Who by Snakes.
In school when they talk about Thanksgiving,
no one even mentions God. Just Indians and pilgrims.

You never knew there could be a holiday
not commanded by God to celebrate, a holiday
not about remembering a miracle like Chanukah
when enough oil for just one night lasted for eight
in a Temple guarded by a small tribe. A family
standing up to an army. Or Purim when Queen Esther
stopped the hanging of the Jews by Haman.
The Red Sea parting, another miracle. A bush
that would not stop burning on top of Mount Sinai,
where Moses got the Ten Commandments
on stone tablets he broke the first time around
because of the sin of worshipping a golden calf.

Sins. Then miracles. More sins. Then thanking God
for forgiving his sinning people even though
they don't deserve it. Those are the holidays you know.
Not one when people stick paper feathers to things
even their behinds, and walk around saying
Gobble not *God*. Laugh. Have days off from school,
but not to walk miles to the synagogue
to stand for hours under a heavy blanket of prayers,
you almost never bored, your brother always.

You don't know what American children
do at home on Thanksgiving besides eat turkey with gravy
and apple pies. Their grandmothers and grandfathers will
be there, you hear them say. Your grandparents
are dead. Killed by Hitler. Long before that
they had to stop celebrating their holidays
unless they sneaked them.
To light a Chanukah candle, small as a crayon,
was a sin to be killed for. To have matzo.
To pray wrapped in a *tallis*.
Sins against Hitler, not God.

There's so much you don't understand. Like God not
bringing miracles to stop Hitler. Or a holiday
about turkeys when people are just happy
and no one is thinking about
God.

Recess again. The boys playing dodgeball. The girls
jumping rope. *Cinderella dressed in yella, how many times
did you kiss your fella? One. Two. Three. Four.*
They don't ask you to jump.
You stare up at the row of birds on a wire,
high toward the sky. Next to each other like friends.

Mrs. Rousin is around the corner of the building and can't see
what is about to happen again on the hard playground.
How some kids will gather round you because
it's recess. First they'll pull off your warm hat, throw it
in a muddy puddle, step on it a lot of times until it gets soaked.
Then one of them will grab it. Force it back on your head.
After that is when they knock you down, pull your skirt over your face.
They'll shout *See the little Jew who comes to school without
panties.* Your face covered with your skirt,
you will hear not see them laughing hard.

The first few times you yelled *I do have panties on!
These are flesh color tights.* But they
yelled louder and you gave up trying to tell the truth.
You asked your mother for different color tights but
she said *No* then *Why?* You didn't
tell her why, so she wouldn't go back to Poland in her mind
and remember worse things than kids making fun.
Kids she'd say just to *ignore* and your daddy would say
to punch. But you don't do either thing.
You tried *Just Ignore Them.* It didn't work.
Ignoring doesn't change a thing. They know
you can hear them. That what they do makes you sad.
And you aren't strong enough to punch so many of them.

Now, a few fourth graders mixed in with third and
some second from your grade come toward you,
faces scrunched up mean, ready to bother the little Jew
who never fights back. You feel your face get hot,
which usually doesn't happen. *Red hot.*
Like something inside you is about to explode.
One of them shoves your shoulder. Another pushes your back.
What they always do to get ready to knock you over. But this time
your legs don't wobble like usual. Instead, they become like steel.

You stand up straighter. Taller. You think of
what your daddy hollers when he has no more patience,
when you better leave him alone or else.
Hak mir nisht in dem chinek arahn!

They won't understand it in Yiddish, so quick you
think of how to say it in English.

STOP BANGING ME ON MY TEAKETTLE!

You holler it just like your daddy does except in English.
Order them to stop. *Now.*
To leave you alone. *Not one more word.*
Not one more push.

Just once is enough when your daddy hollers it.
But you yell it one extra time to make sure they hear you.
Even stamp your foot.
STOP BANGING ME ON MY TEAKETTLE!

The loud angry way you yelled it, not only one time but two,
means they *will* listen and finally leave you alone. They
will know you mean it, will know how much you hate

when they take your hat, tease about your tights
and all the other things, just because
you are Jewish, not a regular American like them.

For a second, they're surprised and don't do anything. Then
one of them shouts *Don't bang me on my teakettle! On my teakettle!*
The little Jew has a teakettle. They laugh so hard they hold their bellies,
can hardly catch their breath, yelling the words over and over
like they are not the angriest thing a person can holler.
But instead like it was a funny thing.
A joke.

Maybe you said it wrong. You must have said it the wrong way,
so instead of them seeing how angry you are and how strong
and leaving you alone, they are making fun of something else
Jewish about you. How you say American expressions wrong. Get things
mixed up. Let Yiddish words and ways of saying things slip in.

When your mother asks how your tights got torn, how they
got blood on them, you say you tripped. *It didn't hurt at all.*
But maybe, you ask carefully as you can, you should get red tights
Instead? Just in case you fall again? She shakes her head.
Dabs mercurochrome on your naked knees. *Just be careful*
not to fall. Then, while she puts the little bottle
into the medicine cabinet, *Maybe red tights someday.*
Maybe for a special occasion.

You never yell again that they should stop banging on your teakettle.
You don't know how
to make them leave you alone. To stop their teasing.
Disappearing seems the best idea.
But for that you would need a miracle. And if God
didn't give miracles to your grandmothers when they were

forced into gas chambers, why would he give one

to a girl in second grade in America

who is only

getting knocked down.

Most people don't know, even your sister who has a doll,
that dolls are real, not dead toys without feelings. That's why
you're mad at Shelly for writing all over her Raggedy Ann
with a green magic marker, even her face, then leaving her
out in the rain to get soaked like a rag and almost dead.
Just because her name is Raggedy doesn't mean she likes
to be treated like a rag, you try to tell your sister.
But she doesn't listen.

You know dolls can love stronger than people.
Kathy loves you more than anyone in the
whole wide world loves you. Always. No matter what.
Kathy knows every single thing that happens to you.
That Kathy can't talk like a person doesn't matter.
She doesn't have to. You and Kathy
talk without out-loud words. You just
think things to each other.
When you feel warm tears roll from your eyes,
Kathy feels them too, her face pressed so close to yours.
To listen. To whisper. To kiss your tears.
She can taste the salt in them.
She feels all the things you feel.
But you don't need to worry. Because Kathy's love
is big as the ocean and she won't break
from too much hurt.

In school, you think of Kathy home by your pillow.
Just waiting there. How when you get back, you will
rush to tell her what happened. Even though she already knows.
How she'll hug you. Will tell you that you *don't stink*.
And Kathy *can* smell things, so she's not just saying you don't.

Besides, Kathy always tells the truth. She's the most honest
patient, kind, brave person you know, who's not exactly
a person. But she *is* alive. And she always
always understands.

Kathy doesn't believe you're selfish. She doesn't ever say
you are too sad. Too afraid. Too mad.
Too happy. Things your mother says.

It doesn't bother Kathy that your parents,
and probably every other grown-up can't tell
she is real. It's better, she says,
for keeping secrets.

When Hot Dog Thursdays start, yours is the only skinny
brown one in the long row of chubby
pink Oscar Mayer Wieners you think come from the fat blimp
that flies over Atlantic City in the summer.
Every Thursday, you bring your wrinkly Kosher frank
wrapped in aluminum foil. Two slices of pumpernickel
in a wax paper bag.
The rest of the kids point at your shriveled frankfurter. Laugh.
Pretend to throw up.

One morning, Mrs. Rousin writes a new word in big letters
on the blackboard. *PREJUDICE.* She starts talking about
respecting differences. Says: *One example is that
people eat different foods, which doesn't make them—*
Stinky! someone calls out. Mrs. Rousin can't
get the class to stop laughing.

She sends home a mimeographed letter, blue ink on pink paper,
for every second grader to give to their parents. Except you.
An invitation to a *Meeting about Respecting Differences.*

That night Mrs. Rousin calls your parents, explains in a kind way
why it might be better for them not to come to the meeting.
After hanging up the black phone on the kitchen wall,
your daddy laughs, says they should all just
Nem a foos unter dem ahrm, un gey cacken oyfen yam.
They should just grab their feet under their arms and
go make caca on the ocean. *Except for Mrs. Rousin,* you don't say
but think it. And Helen who never laughs at your tights or
your cold, wrinkly frankfurter.

After the meeting it all gets worse. The ganging up at recess.
The searching for your Jew-devil horns and finding them
even faster. You wish Mrs. Rousin never got the idea
to teach the parents about differences so they would
teach their children. It just makes them meaner.
But you're also happy. Because now you're sure
Mrs. Rousin doesn't think Jews are bad and dirty.
She even hugs you one morning on the playground
after your knees get scraped by a bunch of third graders
pushing you down. She wants to make things better.
She just doesn't know how.

Red hair. Freckles. Buck teeth. Shy like you.
Helen is the only one who doesn't laugh, who never yells *PU*.
Instead, she lowers her head.
When the rest tease she looks like it hurts her. Like she's sorry
about what they do,
about how you feel.

One day out of the blue she hands you a note
from her mother Mrs. Huck to yours in careful cursive.
Would you like to come to her house for a visit?
A gigantic surprise. Not only the note—
a wish come true you didn't even dare to wish—
but a surprise on top of that when your mother says
it's okay for you to go.

When you get there, Mrs. Huck opens the door,
smiles like she's happy you came. The first
Christian house you ever visited.
She puts an orange on a paper napkin.
Says kindly *I know your people have dietary laws*
I hope this is okay. You nod.
Mrs. Huck says *dietary laws* like it's alright to
have them. Even though they make you so different.
No Oscar Mayer hotdogs. No ketchup, mustard, or
baked beans without the Kosher U. Can't roast
marshmallows because of gelatin from pigs in them.

But none of that matters while you slowly peel your
orange. The first time you peel one all by yourself.
It's the sweetest, most delicious, most orange
orange you ever ate. Probably, ever will eat.

Sucking its juice, you feel like you can taste Helen's
shyness. Mrs. Huck's kindness.
Happiness tears rush into your eyes. You try
to keep them from spilling out. Put the peels
in a neat pile on the white paper napkin.
You want to say thank you
with your whole life, not just
two words.

Mother in Dick, Jane, and Sally's house bakes cookies and
never gets mad. Just like the mother in *Father Knows Best.*
You would give anything for a mother like that. A sin to wish,
you know. So you make sure to keep it a secret
while you keep wishing for a not-so-angry, not-so-sad mother
to put a plate of chocolate chip cookies on the kitchen table
after school. To smile while she pours the milk.

Father in Dick, Jane, and Sally goes to work wearing
a suit and a tie that he doesn't just save for synagogue.
Because *Father* never goes to synagogue. Or to parties.
And never drinks schnapps. *Father* carries
a briefcase. Not wire baskets full of eggs.
He doesn't worry all the time about
not having enough money. Doesn't wake up
screaming from nightmares. There are even times
Father is not working. He fixes things.
Doesn't try to be the boss of Dick, Jane, and Sally.
Father in the book never spanks.

Jane has golden yellow hair like
most of the girls in your school. Not dark like yours.
She wears dresses that are never dirty.
Doesn't cry under her pillow.

Puff doesn't try to scratch Spot's eyes out like your drunk neighbor's
wild cat who made your German shepherd Lucky bleed.

Dick is quiet. Never hunts cockroaches in the kitchen
like Marty does.

Sally looks and acts a lot like your little sister Shelly.
You don't like either of them. Sally or your sister.
Mother and *Father* don't pick Sally to be their favorite.
They like all three of their children. Your parents
like Shelly the best. They never holler at her.
She's skinny and they don't want her to be.
So they do all sorts of things to make her eat.
When Uncle Avrom visits from Israel he gives Shelly
the name *Kushera Fudom*. Sacred thread. To show
she is skinny *and* special. Which is why
they never spank her.

Like that time your mother was in the coops
and Shelly colored on the brand-new light gray
wall-to-wall carpet in the living room where
no one is allowed except for company (that almost never comes).
Your mother saw the scribbling. Same time you saw it.
Crayons spread all around.
And where were you? she screamed, starting to look wild.
She slapped your face. Hit you on your arm, yelling
it was your fault for not watching your sister better.
A scratch from her long red fingernails
made a bubble of blood drop on the new carpet next to the other colors.
Your mother wouldn't stop hitting and screaming about their first ever
carpet spoiled. All because of *a selfish little girl*
who didn't take care of her sister like she should.
She screamed until your daddy came in from the coops and
pulled her away from you.
Hugged her tight. Told her it would be okay.
They would clean the carpet. Told you with his eyes
to go somewhere else.

Dick, Jane, and Sally have *Grandmother* and *Grandfather*.
You don't. Never did. Never will.

Everything in Dick, Jane, and Sally's house is different from yours.
The biggest difference being:
in their house everyone is happy.
Maybe it's because they don't have a War to remember.
Don't need to worry
about what might happen next
if they aren't extra careful.

I see you in your bedroom. Lights out,
your brother snoring in the next bed
head-to-head with yours. Nightly, he
drifts away mid-whisper leaving you
alone again. Your little sister still, until
she dreams. Warm tears roll slowly
from the corners of your open eyes. Enough
to wet the pillow with your soundless crying
in that room with three beds and the old wall piano.
Nothing else but the narrow closet
where a few clothes hang. Mouse turds
under the stool you stand on to reach a blouse.

Why you cry is bigger than any one thing.
The teasing that never stops. How they smell your skin
and scream *PU*. How it seems impossible
to become invisible, no matter how hard you wish it.
How even in your small farmhouse
you are not safe from attack. Mean, too.
Just different. Being a Jew seems a curse,
which is probably a sin to even think. A thought
that will get chased out with a belt
if they find it in your mind.

You get up, tiptoe to your bedroom door,
listen to your mother crying in the kitchen, your daddy
cursing in Yiddish over the whirr of the Singer sewing machine.
Again, it's about the fall in the price of eggs
killing the small chicken farmers. How will we
keep this fahshthinkenna farm? Where will we go?
Nobody wants us. Each word a sorrow.

Sorrow after sorrow stitched into the new
blouse they are making for you to wear to school.

You walk softly back to your bed
away from the crack between the door and wall where
without them knowing you watch your daddy's eyes get
so red with tears, most nights he has to take off his glasses
to wipe them so he can see to sew.

BABY CHICKS

A whole bunch got delivered while you were still sleeping.
You hear them the minute you come into coop number 7—
where the baby chicks got put under big round hoods
that look like flying saucers and keep them warm.
Too many chicks to even count.
Before you step any closer, you close your eyes to hear better
the sound they make all together. A song like nothing else.

You wish your daddy didn't have to vaccinate them.
One by one by one. Their small, soft, warm, yellow bodies
scooped up, not just for holding close and loving.
He says he needs your help. Asks you to give him
one chick at a time for him to put the needle in.
Says it's good for them, even if they are little and scared.

They try to get away when you reach for them.
Your daddy laughs, shows you how to move faster,
not be afraid to grab one.
They won't break.
You start to pick them up better. Feel each baby's heart
beat in your hands. Its scrambly little legs tickle your palms.
You hold each warm round chick close to you,
whisper *Don't be afraid*
right before you give it up.

After a whole bunch are done,
so many you and your daddy are both tired, he leaves.
You stay. Sit down in the straw
by the pen with chicks who already got a needle.
Tell them you are sorry. You hope it didn't hurt too much,
wish they could stay well without a needle stuck in

just under their tiny wings where your daddy said
it wouldn't hurt. And maybe it really didn't
because now they are carefree, playing, running around,
pecking at things you can't see.
Even if he's not right and it did hurt,
they are still singing.

You lie back in the straw. Close your eyes.
Rest in baby chick heaven
even if it won't stay this way because
you'll have to go back to the house,
and they
will grow into chickens.

Pouring rain. Your favorite kind of day. You find the deepest puddle.
At first, just watch the drops land. Then, down low on your belly, you
set leaf boats floating. Blow to give them wind. An ocean full of boats.

How can you resist? You take off one sock then the other. Step in.
A giant among the floating boats. You don't sink them. Just sit.
Your wet hair drips tiny rivers into your eyes. Water balloons your shorts.
Your soaked blouse stuck to your back, your nipples. *Off with them all!*
Shorts. Blouse. Even your panties tossed into the drenched green grass.

Naked now. You, a hippopotamus stretched out in muddy water,
a thirsty hippo who can't drink this, like the clear water at A Lion's Beach.
The hippo rolls over. Starts catching raindrops, clean because they
drop from the sky on his large wide tongue.

You sit up. A mermaid now. Stir the puddle bottom with your hands.
Make muddy puddle soup. The mermaid's *peshy* under brown water.
Her shimmery tail hidden. You scoop a clump of mud. Pretend it's soap.
A girl again, you stand, rub mud on your legs, your arms, think this
is how to change the color of your skin, but not really
because the rain washes it off. You sit back down. Press and roll mud
between leaves to make mud sandwiches, small stones stuck in
for extra flavor. You pretend eat. Feel hungry for a real sandwich.
Stand up and get ready to be done. You stomp hard. Splash like crazy,
shrinking the puddle ocean because of the water you make escape.
You try to shake off like your dog Lucky. Step out of the ocean.
Pick up your wet, muddy-now-like-you clothes.
Mud shampoo still in your hair. Mud between your toes.
Mud soap on your belly.

You walk slow. Catch more raindrops on your tongue.
A duck waddling home.
You pull open the screen door. Drop your soaked clothes, shoes,
everything but yourself, in the small foyer where you're
supposed to leave muddy things before
coming all the way into the house.

Isn't she too old for this? you hear your daddy say to your mother
soon as you come into the kitchen. She puts her finger to her lips
like he should be quiet. Shakes her head.
Let her play, Arnold. One day, she'll outgrow mud puddles.
She smiles at you. *Let her be a child.*

She wets a washcloth in the sink, gets a towel and right there
in the middle of the kitchen cleans off the mud,
making a tiny puddle by your feet.

Your daddy doesn't say anything else, doesn't argue
that she's wrong to let you, a girl who's already seven,
play naked in a mud puddle for such a long time that
she looks like a wrinkled prune. He goes back to his newspaper.
Shakes his head like he doesn't understand your mother.
Or you.

After you are dry and dressed, your mother tells you
about the time before The War when she was
sitting on the step outside her house in Kraznystav, playing
with a doll. She was older than you are now.
Maybe eleven or twelve. A neighbor stopped.
Scolded her. *What are you doing, foolish girl?*
Playing with a doll like you are just a child?
Like your father isn't dead. Like the Nazis aren't taking over.

Don't you know you are too old to play with dolls?
What a fool!

I never forgot, she says. Not looking at you anymore,
but at that neighbor, her doll, the steps of that long-ago house
and the people who used to live inside it.
I don't want that to happen to you, she says,
her voice drifting away as she slips from the kitchen, from you,
from her smile when you, dripping wet and muddy,
stepped naked into the house and
she seemed happy for you.

I see you on the way to the bus stop trying to make it past
the earthworms covering the shiny dark road wet with rain.
You try so hard not to squish any. It takes such concentration
walking next to your little brother who tries to squish them on purpose.
As many as he can. You tell him not to. But he won't listen,
won't be careful. You don't think he can hear the sound they make,
how they cry out when they get stepped on,
when their life is squeezed out by someone's shoe.
You don't like how slimy they are, but still, you don't want to kill them.

There are so so many of them. Too many to count.
You twist your foot sideways not to step on any. Take very short
and extra-long steps to put your foot down where none are.
Cover your ears not to hear their strange screams.

When you try to teach Marty how not to step on them
he does the opposite. Tries harder to land on one.
You holler at him to make him stop. But he's laughing and doesn't care.
Or doesn't understand. Like that time he threw every one of Lucky's
new puppies, born in the back of the old green pickup, off the truck
because he wanted to give them to Lucky. One by one
they hit the ground and died. Lucky made sad sounds,
licked her puppies. But didn't bite Marty.
You wanted to push him off the back of the pickup truck
so he would feel what it was like. But you didn't dare.
Because what if you killed him too? Anyway, it was your fault
for not stopping him in time.

Now you can't stop him from jumping on the earthworms,
whose life is squishing out. You feel a little bit like throwing up,
but you better not, because if you do, you'll have to turn around

and walk all the way back home on the earthworm covered road.
Then, after getting cleaned up, you'll have to come back and,
because Marty is so little, you will have to bring him with you both ways
while he keeps stepping on the worms. The whole morning
will be like one of your earthworm nightmares come true
when Iona Road is pitch dark and covered with crawling worms,
and you can't keep from stepping on them.

I see you at the bus stop, the butterflies in your belly
getting wilder because Terry will be here soon.
You look down at the sand under your feet,
happy it's sunny because the tiny diamonds shine.
If Terry ever talked to you, you would tell her about the diamonds.
Maybe both of you would kneel down together, look closer.
You could sift the sand in your hands. Find the hiding
diamonds. Be happy together about treasure in ordinary sand.

Most days, Terry comes when there aren't too many minutes left
before the driver who never smiles will stop at the corner,
pull the handle to open the doors and say *Good morning* to Terry,
the first to climb up, with no good morning for you and Marty.

On her way to the bus stop now, Terry is holding her nose
because you stink so much even from far away.
PU a Jew, she yells. Like she does every day
except for when there is no school or when she's absent.
You tell Marty to get behind you.
Even though you're still mad about him killing earthworms,
you won't let Terry do mean things to him.
He's only in kindergarten.
PU Two Jews, she shouts. *What a GIGANTIC stink.*
She repeats *STINK STINK STINK*, which comes out funny
because she's holding her nose. But you don't laugh.

When Terry gets closer, you step back, hold
Marty's arms wrapped around your waist
like you're one person with four legs backing up.
As far back as you can go without being in the road.
You can tell Terry is collecting spit in her mouth

for her first huge gob. You have to be ready to move fast
when she blows it out of her mouth.

Her big slimy saliva ball just misses
the tip of your red corrective shoe. The next one almost
hits your lunchbox, but you jump out of the way just in time.
Madder now because she's missing, Terry spits the next one
like it's poison. You think maybe it went in your hair
but don't want to reach up and find out.

MotherfuckinsonofabitchbastarddirtyfilthyJewbitch. Now
Terry spits her poison words. You understand *dirty filthy Jew.*
The rest are American *curse words.* You know because
your mother told you, crying while she did, when you
tried to repeat the words to her. You never did again
because of how she squeezed the kitchen towel so tight
and her eyes got their faraway look. Like she was hearing
her neighbors in Poland call her *Dirty Jew* and curse her for
killing Jesus Christ. *Jews didn't do that,* your mother says.
*Why would we kill Jesus? They just wanted to find
something else to blame us for. They were always
looking to blame us.*

You wonder if Terry thinks you killed Jesus. If she asked,
you would tell her you don't even know who Jesus is.
That you never killed anything. Well. Except for cockroaches.
And some ants. Oh. And that mouse.
But you didn't kill it on purpose.
It died by itself in your tights.

Goodfornothingbastardmotherfuckincuntfaceslut.
Good for nothing are the words you understand this time. And *face.*
Terry's eyes narrow. She makes her hands into claws. Bends down
and grabs a fist of sand. She doesn't even think

about the diamonds in it.
With the sand in her claw fist, Terry comes so close
you can feel her breath that smells kind of rotten. You don't
dare move. Besides there's nowhere to go but into the road.
Terry pulls your collar away from your neck with one claw.
Pours the sand that's in the other claw down your back.
It doesn't sting exactly. Just feels strange.
Uncomfortable. *Wrong.* Because sand down your back
between your blouse and skin doesn't belong there.
She grabs more sand. Forces it down your back.
You want to cry. Press your lips together hard.

How Terry gets reminds you of the mean scratching cat
that sneaks into your farm and as soon as it sees Lucky
hunches its back. Its claws come out. Tail like a twisty wire arrow.
Hissing and spitting, it attacks Lucky who,
even though she's a big German shepherd and could kill that cat,
doesn't.
If you tried to fight, to force sand down Terry's back, you couldn't.
She is bigger. A fourth grader. And besides, you don't
want to fight with Terry. You want Terry to want to be your friend,
the only girls around here on roads with hardly any houses.
But it's no use.

❧ SCHOOL BUS

The long yellow bus comes. Stops. Doors open.
You follow Terry up the steps into more teasing.
You hate the school bus, even though you're not
allowed to say hate or even to think it except
about the Nazis and Hitler, *yemach shmo,* erased be his name.
But you *do* hate what happens most days on the yellow bus.
How the kids search your hair for horns because
their parents told them Jews are devils.
The horns they always find are *proof,* they yell.
The best days are when they forget to tease, when
by magic they ignore you because they
got excited about something else. Which is almost never.
On the bus, Donna Fagliarini is in charge of the teasing.
She's the only other girl at Jacksonville School besides you
who has dark hair and a thick long ponytail. But
she's Italian, so it's okay.

You learn it's better to keep secret
what happens at the bus stop and in the yellow bus.
Another secret in the pile of secrets in your mind
where you hope your mother won't ever find them.

When she tells your daddy about the curse words,
you are afraid he will go fight with Terry's father or
make you force sand down Terry's back, because
he doesn't want cowards for children.
But before he can say anything, your mother gets up.
She takes off her apron and standing up straight as a broom,
commands, *You just need to ignore her, my daughter.*
Repeat after me: Sticks and stones
may break my bones, but words
will never hurt me.
Her first saying in English.

She makes you learn it by heart.
But it's not true, you don't say. Words *do hurt.*
They feel like sand sliding down your back,
sticking to your skin. With no way to get them off you.

❧ SWING

You lean back. Hands tight on the chains.
Legs stretched out in front, pointing skyward. You lift.
Bend your knees back quick. Lean forward. Swing back.
Lift again. Hold on tight. Your body a rocket.
You pump pump pump. Mount higher and higher
until you fly so high and hard,
one tall metal back leg lifts off the ground.
Then the front leg when you swing back.
The rear leg up again when you soar forward,
like a giant starting to walk, one heavy step at a time
across the farm to who knows where.

Your brother down below warning
Be careful you'll make it tip over!

You just laugh. Lean back. Go higher.
The giant moves because of how strong you are.
How free. Nobody can reach you.
Like you are a bird. *No. Even freer.*
A girl with wings.

Your back against the willow's wide strong trunk.
Back-to-back with your best friend. You have three.
Kathy your doll. Lucky your dog. And the willow.
Three best friends who don't talk with words, but even better.

You hope your mother won't squeak open the screen door.
Won't holler for you. You want to stay and feel the wind,
another friend, comb the willow's long green hair and
play with yours. Nothing is better than this. Your hand
resting on Lucky's warm back, the willow over both of you.

The wind makes the willow dance wild. She doesn't need
vodka to get happy and dance, to wiggle, to wave her many arms.

You know not to tell anyone besides Kathy that
you can hear the willow laugh and cry.
Lucky already knows because Lucky hears her like you do.
Raindrops are her tears sometimes. She also cries with small leaves
falling, twirling to the ground.
When she gets sad, which is not very often,
you try to cheer her up. And you do when you come close,
lean against her. Both of you feel better right away.
Her trunk gets straighter. Makes you get that way.
You feel her breathing. The two of you breathe together.
Lucky breathing with you.

You wish you could be her. Be a willow tree.
She doesn't ever have to go anywhere. Her roots keep her
right where she is. She never leaves her spot.
She doesn't do bad things that make people holler at her.
She doesn't have to *not be shy*.

Doesn't have to dress up and go to birthday parties
for other *greena*'s children who she hardly knows.
But the luckiest thing of all: the willow tree doesn't ever
have to wait for a school bus. She just gets to stay
right where she grows. Under the sky.
Day sky. Night sky.
Near the swing set. The picnic table. The clothesline.
The empty bungalow with the broken door.
Being kind of close to the cesspool doesn't bother her
because she's a tree. Quiet and alone as she wants to be.
A willow who talks without words. To you.

You picked your best friend Kathy's name
because of kind Kathy Adams, the once-in-a-blue-moon
babysitter who is fourteen, lives around the corner
near the creek and doesn't act like Jews stink.

Kathy brings storybooks to read every time.
Pats a spot next to her, one side for you,
the other for your brother. Your sister on her lap.
Kathy Adams doesn't mind touching and even
hugging you all.
She sings while she tucks you in. Like she's happy
to be there, happy to make diamond-shaped
peanut butter and jelly sandwiches without
scrunching her nose at the bread, rye with caraway seeds
or pumpernickel, the only kinds in your house. But
Kathy never says *PU*.

You want to be Kathy Adams when you grow up.
When you tell her, she smiles, says
Who will be Annie then?

Shaped like a teepee.
It stands up on its own in the middle of your bedroom.

Your mother got it on sale at J. C. Penney for you to wear to
birthday parties in Vineland that you don't like going to.
The dressing up, ankle socks, patent leather shoes not good for
your turned-in ankles, the kids who all go to the same happy school.
But maybe having your own crinoline—
layered like a wedding cake you once saw in a bakery,
white like fresh snowflakes, and stiff enough to stand alone—
is worth a once-in-a-while birthday.

You get down on your belly, slide under the bottom layer.
Squat inside. Wait (quiet as a crinoline when it's not moving),
to surprise Marty. The crinoline, a volcano.
You, lava.

I see you heading to the clothesline barefoot, the grass
so full of morning dew, the wet squeezes up between your toes.
Your arms out wide to reach the handles of the big laundry basket
pressed against your belly, the smell of wet washed sheets
better than almost any smell except for maybe lilacs.
This is a job you love, even though it's not one bit easy
to get those big white sheets over the clothesline.
It's good you have *a system*.

You set the basket on the grass.
Reach into the clothespin bag hanging on the line.
Grab three of the wood clothespins. Put them between your teeth.
Tuck others into a pocket if you have one and if not,
keep the hanging bag close enough to reach. Then
you gather a bundle of twisted sheet, heave it over the line.
You patiently untwist and untwist until it hangs open in the sun
like a huge wet blank sheet of paper.

On windy days, your face gets slapped a lot, but it doesn't hurt.
It makes you smile. How the wet clean sheet presses into you.
How if the wind is strong, the sheet hugs you
so that not only your face but your bare arms and
even your legs get wrapped in the wet sheet.

On days without fighting winds when half a sheet, or almost half
is over the line then even without clothespins holding it down,
that sheet will not undo itself, will not fool you. But until then,
while only an edge is over the line with the rest
on the opposite side, you have to be so quick on your feet,
fast with your hands, with your seeing.

There is no place you would rather be.
When you stare up at the sun, which you can't help when you
reach high to pull the line down, to clip on the clothespins,
the sun's flashing light is part of the magic.
Everything is full of light and play. The way the wind teases and
just when you think you are going to get that sheet over, the wind
pushes back. How the sun makes the clothesline seem to be
in two places at once and you bring a pin down where there is no rope,
just a line of light. Everything is laughing at you,
but it doesn't bother you. You laugh at you too.

Everything is so much more alive than your parents know.
They wouldn't believe you if you told them. *It's just*
your imagination, they would say. That you imagine too much.
But sheets are real. Laundry baskets are real. Clothespins
and clotheslines and wet grass too—dew being part magic.
Toes are real and the sky in which the sun lives.
Though sky and sun and clouds are more magic than the rest,
being so far and out of reach.

Finally you are finished hanging not only the sheets,
but also your daddy's *hemdellas,* his sleeveless undershirts
and the panties and the socks that are your least favorite to hang,
because you always run out of clothespins and have to double things up.

You back up, sit down in the wet grass.
Watch the wind blow the sheets like huge flags,
but not red, white, and blue with lots of stars.
These are *your* flags. They wave in *your* land of the free.
They don't stand for America which is only sort of free.
You sit for a long time. Hope your mother will not call you.
Because now comes the best part.

Now is when you start to see the angels,
who only come when your hands are out of the way.
They're made of light.
Tiny sparkling tightrope walkers appearing and disappearing,
sparkling on and off.
They wear lace petticoats and tights of all colors,
bounce on the clothesline, do somersaults, play angel leapfrog.
You can hear them laughing from where you watch on your belly now,
not too far away but far enough so they know they are safe,
that they will be left alone.

Their laughing is, you think, what dew would sound like
if it could laugh and if you could hear it laughing.
Or maybe not. Dew would be quieter probably.
The angels on the clothesline are noisy,
their laughter like millions of tiny bells.
Tiny bells no one could ever count.
Just like no one can see the angels.
They let you see and hear them, maybe because they know
you would never hurt them or tell anyone about them.

You hope they will never hide from you.
You tell them in your mind that you are so happy to see them.
That you wish you could become small and magic enough
to dance with them, to play with them on the clothesline,
to be as happy and free and invisible as they are.

It's about three girls. Two of them
don't want to be friends with the other one.
They whisper about her. Mean things.
Laugh at her. Tell other kids to do it too.
She's kind anyway. Tries to be friends with them.
Wants to be.
But they just laugh. Turn their backs.

She is sad. But
not surprised.

Then partway through the story,
you, the one writing it,
realize.
You are the one making up the story so
in a way you are like God is to the world.
You can make
anything happen.

So you do. You change one of the girls.
Change her mind.

She starts talking to the girl
she pushed away at first.
Stops being mean to her. Decides
she *does* want to be that girl's friend
after all. The whole story,
the whole world in the story,
changes.

In the end
all three girls
are friends.

That is the day you feel for the first time
power you didn't know was yours.
Even though you can't
make anyone
want to be your friend in real life,
you *can* in your stories.
There is no end
to the good things you can make happen
in worlds you create.

Penciling words
that smear on the blue-lined page,
you see,
clear as
the loops and curves of the letters,
what you want
to do
forever.

To start *Shabbos* off on Friday night, your mother lights the candles.
Right at the *Candle Lighting Time* printed in the Yiddish newspaper.
You stand at the doorway to the kitchen that doesn't have a door.
Watch her from behind. See her move her arms in front of her
like she is trying to bring something invisible close.
She makes a bowl with her hands,
lowers her face into her cupped palms. Stays like that,
whispering to God.
When she lifts her head, her eyes are red. Full of tears.
Good Shabbos, she says.
Kisses your daddy first. Then you, Marty, Shelly.

Sometimes she hurries to the silver menorah wearing just her panties,
not even her brassiere, her *chitchis* hanging loose.
She quick covers her head with a paper napkin.
Strikes the match. Lights the candles. Those days
you wonder how she is not embarrassed
to stand in front of God that way.
Being late to light the candles must be worse.
You ask God to forgive her for coming to the candles almost naked.
You imagine clothes on her while she lights
then whispers to God. Face hidden in her hands.

I.

Your mother wants Saturdays here to be *how Shabbos was back home.*
Before the Nazis. No matter how many tsuros, worries
a person had during the week, they disappeared on *Shabbos,* she says.
Sabbath was a day everybody was rich. Nobody went to work, to school.
No one carried money. Delicious food was prepared ahead of time because
nobody cooked that day. The mothers and the bubas
were like queens on Shabbos. My father sang to my mother
every Friday night when he came home from synagogue
that she was more precious to him than rubies and gold.
Everybody wore their best clothes and for those who
did not have nice clothes or enough food, others made sure to provide.
We took care of each other. That's how it was. Heaven on earth.

She says *Shabbos* morning started with praying together,
reading the Torah, then continued with *only other good things.*
Like the children playing in the square,
the parents close by. Enjoying themselves. A time for not
being angry at the Reboina Shel Olam for what He doesn't give.
Instead counting the blessings of what He does give. Imagine.

II.

She wishes now her children would be in the little Elmer synagogue
on *Shabbos.* With the Torah. But that hardly ever happens.
Most Saturday mornings, you wake up and watch cartoons.
Not only that. You get to choose which cereal box you want
with the little doors that open and wax paper inside that keeps the milk
from leaking out. You convince Marty the Special K and Wheaties are
the yummiest. Keep the Frosted Flakes and Sugar Smacks for yourself.

You sister gets what's left. If she's lucky Raisin Bran.
You all eat, watching cartoons up close to the television, turned down
low on the glassed-in porch next door to your parents' little bedroom,
where they are still in bed because the Torah says a husband and wife
should kiss on *the Sabbath*.
You try to chew quietly, tell your brother and sister to chew quietly too,
so you won't disturb them. Maybe that's why your mother
doesn't make everyone go to synagogue. Because she likes
not being disturbed for a change. And kissing your daddy.

III.

Except for making *Kiddush*, blessing the wine on Friday night, your
daddy doesn't keep *Shabbos* the way your mother wants him to. Instead, he
takes you and Marty with him to Elmer, lets you ride in the back of the old
green pickup, standing up, your hair blowing wild while he drives fast
because your mother isn't there to say *Please stop speeding, Arnold*.
He loves driving fast as much as you and Marty love him to go fast.
Sometimes he turns the corner quick on purpose to trick you both,
making you fall on top of each other laughing. You keep all this secret
from your mother who wishes your daddy wouldn't drive on the Sabbath,
wouldn't go to the bank or pick that day to go to the Barber Shop.
But you are glad he does and that he brings you along.

IV.

In Elmer with two quarters in your pocket, you walk all by yourself from
the Barber Shop with the spinning thing that reminds you of a candy
cane to the Elmer 5 & 10, whose name stands for a nickel and dime and is
your favorite inside place. A bell rings as soon as you open the door
to walk on the wood floors that creak in a special way like nowhere else.
Inside there are so many different smells. Together they turn into one
that is exactly the Elmer 5 & 10 smell.
When the lady with the ruffled apron who usually stands

behind the counter in the middle of the store, doesn't call out hello,
you guess she has a customer. The sound of the cash register drawer
shooting open proves it.   You go straight to the potholder loops.

You have to decide whether to choose the big bag of potholder loops
with a bunch of colors but the loops kind of raggedy and different sizes.
Or two smaller bags with one color in each, all the loops the same size
and nicer. You take a long time deciding. Finally pick one bag of orange,
one bright blue. Both together cost one of the quarters
you got from Franya Hertz who bought two potholders from you
for one quarter each. She is your best customer even though
you hardly ever visit her. The other quarter left over is for candy.
Another secret from your mother that you keep with your daddy.

Usually you pick nonpareils, malted balls, and Almond Joy. But only
if you have enough left over because Almond Joy costs a whole dime.
It's worth it. Never jawbreakers or anything peppermint like Marty
picks when you bring him along. You don't know which lady it will be
today behind the counter with the rows of candy. The one who acts like
you should hurry up or the other one who smiles and is patient.
Like she understands that when a person can only buy candy.
once in a blue moon, it takes a long time to decide which to pick.

I see you at the wooden picnic table near the swing,
trying to keep your elbows off the table while you eat
your egg salad sandwich. Your mother keeps reminding you,
pushes your elbow away when it rests down on the wood.

Elbows Off the Table is in Amy Vanderbilt's *ETIQUETTE* book
that teaches your mother how to be American. There are even
harder things to do like switch your fork
from one hand to the other and learn the right way to
hold your knife when you cut meat.
But those two things your mother gives up
on making everyone do when your daddy says the Americans can eat
however they want, he's not going to change how he eats.

The picnic table is where they tell about *The War.*
You children should know everything, they both say.
Your mother's only relative who survived, Yakov, a distant cousin,
doesn't agree with them. Yakov argues that it's
too much of a burden for children.
They're too young for such things. So he doesn't tell his children
what happened in The War. *Later, when they are old enough,*
I will tell them.

Your daddy criticizes Yakov behind his back,
apologizing to your mother right before or right after he says
not nice things about the one person in the world related to her
who survived. He calls Yakov a coward. Says he's
making a big mistake.
At the picnic table, your daddy says it's his job
to tell his children about *The War. If we don't, who will?*
It doesn't matter if it's hard to hear about it. Too bad.
It was worse to live through.

So they do tell. Every single time your family eats at the picnic table.
Usually on Saturdays. Usually sandwiches, the easiest thing to
take outside to eat. With sour pickles and sometimes
Frank's Orange Soda for a special treat.
These are not normal American picnics, you are almost sure.

At one picnic your mother tells about her mother sending her away
to save her life before the Nazis would return to Kraznystav
for one last roundup. Your mother was maybe fifteen.
Her mother gave her a chain to wear with a cross, taught her
how to make a cross on her body the way Christians do,
along with the words to say in Polish. She told your mother
not to answer to Esther anymore. She would be Eva
from then on. Her red hair and good Polish would help.
Your mother cries, describing the small sugar cubes
put in her pockets that last time she saw her mother.
Her mother told her the sugar would help dirty water
taste better when she was escaping. She was so thirsty
the next day, she drank from a rusty spout on the side of a barn
she snuck up to late at night, so nobody would see and shoot her.
She used half a cube. A whole sugar cube, the night she drank
from the trough where a farmer's pigs got their water. Drank it
even though pigs aren't Kosher. Because her mother told her
to do anything to stay alive. And she promised she would.

At a picnic of tongue sandwiches on rye bread with mustard,
she starts telling again about the morning her cousin Rifka's baby
was stabbed with a pitchfork. But she can't finish the story that day.

One Sunday, after giving pieces of pastrami to everyone else,
because she can never eat at the picnics, she tells about being hidden
under the floorboards of a barn where she couldn't move her legs.
The Christian man who hid her would come every few days.

If the coast was clear, she could come out for a few minutes.
Stretch her legs. He brought her water and food. News.
She was sure she would be the only Jew left. Wanted to die
more times than can be counted. But she couldn't end her life.
Because of her promise to her mother.

Your daddy stands while he tells his stories. Smiles a lot when he
talks about all the ways he outsmarted death. Starvation. Nazis.
Russians. In the labor camp by the Volga River, men's hands
froze and stuck to shovels. They had to be cut off.
He kept moving, never stopped long enough, no matter how
exhausted he was, to let the freezing happen. Pushed himself to
keep working. He thawed frozen dogs at night not to starve in Siberia.
Forced his brother Maier to take bites until Maier finally
stopped throwing up. *Maier would be dead if not for me.*
You don't like how your daddy talks about people who
didn't have chutzpah like his, who are not like him—
someone who wasn't, who isn't afraid of anything.

You are eating sardines and cream cheese on marbled rye.
But stop when your mother describes a death march passing
through her village a week before she left Kraznystav. Her mother
gave her a piece of bread, told her to run to a woman carrying
two small children, to give her the bread. *Be extra careful,*
her mother said. *Be fast and don't let the guards see you.*

My mother was an angel, your mother says, and cannot stop crying
for a long time. You wish you could help her feel better. But you know
you can't. You stay quiet as you can, almost not breathing
like she had to do under the floor in that barn.

You want to cover your ears, so you won't hear, won't understand
all the things they tell you, the way your little sister doesn't understand
because she's too little and runs off to play with her Raggedy Ann.

But you also want to stay.

Elbows on the table, you lean forward.

Don't want to miss a word at the same time you wish they would stop.

That they didn't have stories like this to tell. That instead they would

tell jokes or different kinds of stories while eating plump hot dogs

in buns smeared with ketchup and mustard. Later, roast marshmallows.

At those picnics, the mother never cries or hollers Yiddish curses.

That mother doesn't even think to check

what's okay with Amy Vanderbilt.

Your daddy screams in the night. Terrified.
So different than how he is in the day.
Your mother whispers *Nunya,*
her tender name for him. *It's okay, Nunya.*
It's the past.
She kisses his tears.
Puts his head in her lap. Strokes his face.
She, the strong one then.

Listening in the hallway, you hold your breath.
Glimpse his red eyes. A sudden stranger without
his thick glasses. Without his strength.

You wait for his crying to stop.
For it to become quiet
in the small farmhouse hiding under kind stars.
It helps knowing they are sparkling up there
where they can't be hurt. Still shining no matter
the darkness. No matter how dark those nights
filling with memories
that haunt your fearless father.

While playing dress-up in their small bedroom,
you find it. In the night-table drawer,
under a shiny black and gold box with rubbery things in it.

A picture of a truckload of arms and legs.
Just arms and legs
piled up in the back of a big pickup.

You listen for your parents to come in from the coops.
Not yet.

You look closer.
Try to figure out which arms belong to your grandmothers,
which to your uncles, only little boys then.
You stare through the tears hurrying to fill your eyes.
You want to see what they saw.
Wish they had hidden this picture
where you couldn't find it.

You never tell them about finding the picture.
Always putting it back just the way it was
under the shiny black and gold box.

I see you ride your blue bicycle into the wind.
Fast as you can pedal. You become an arrow
aiming into the wonderful wind that blows your hair back,
thrills your bare arms and legs.

Your parents don't know, and you don't tell them
how you leave behind the death marches.
The airless cattle cars. The gas chambers.
How you turn your back on the sticks and stones,
the names that hurt at home too.

On your bike you are Annie Oakley.
Guns ready in your holster. One on your left hip,
one on your right. You ride your trusty speedy horse
with its wild mane of pink and blue streamers whipping in the wind.
You are fast and free together that mile to the creek
where you will both go down to drink the sparkling cold water.
Not just free. *Wild* and free.
Out of reach of them blaming you. Them saying
if only you obeyed better they would suffer less.
But no, they complain. *Instead, you have a mind of your own.*
You wish that liking what you like,
not just what your parents want you to like,
wasn't against the Ten Commandments.
Wasn't a kind of sin.

You ride your bike faster into the wind,
wishing it wasn't wrong
to want to be happy. Or a worse sin:
to act carefree.

I.

They would have named you Channah, the name
that belonged to your mother's mother. But Tanta Rae
insisted that in America they should
give you an English name, easy to pronounce.
In a new country you need a new name, new ways,
she told them. *I know about such things. Trust me.*
And they did.
Only months off the boat, what did they know?

So Tanta Rae took charge. Not Hannah. Too old-fashioned.
Ann. That's a good one. My neighbor in 2A told me
it means the same as Channah. Just more modern.

So *Ann* got put on the birth certificate when the nurse asked.
Just above *Shoulder Pads* in the blank by *Father's Occupation*.
Even though they couldn't pronounce Ann.
That American *A* impossible for them.

II.

One day you add a silent *e* to those three letters.
Tell your parents you like it better that way.
Your parents don't know about silent *e*'s. *Ehni*
they start saying when they don't call you *ketsella* or *bubalah*.
Dr. Falheimer and the teacher say *Anne*,
just like they said it before the new *e*,
Like someone pulling a handle attached to you
that you can't feel. But when they pull it,
you should let them in.
But you are not really *Ann* or *Anne* with a silent *e*

and you can't be *Channahla* in America except to Tanta Rae
who never calls you by the name she picked.

III.

Finding out about Annie Oakley changes everything.
You begin writing *Annie* everywhere. Even in school.
Annie almost matches how your parents say it
But most important and best of all, Annie goes with
imagining yourself tough like Annie Oakley.
Not afraid of anybody.

IV.

It will change again one more time.
Children will write *Ani* on the pictures they draw for you
in the bilingual school you open
and name *El Buche del Canguro, A Kangaroo's Pouch*.
Ani because that's how it sounds to them *en español*.
Only three letters. But these just the right ones.
You will like how it looks, how it
sounds when they say it.

At your first meditation retreat,
you won't know what a spiritual name is.
When they ask for one, you write *Ani*.
In meditation, it will come to you that
Ahní in Hebrew means *I Am*.
You won't turn back from Ani after that.

IV.

In your seventh decade, you will make it
legal. Choose the name to put on the certificate.
You will name yourself.

Your parents know *pronunciation* is a big deal if they
want Americans to understand them, even though they can't
pronounce the word *pronunciation* right
or most long English words and a lot of short ones too.

Like that time your mother remembers in Brooklyn,
pregnant with your brother and with the urge for something sweet.
She kept pointing and repeating *Sho-co-lad. Please, shocolad.*
But the girl behind the counter in the candy store shrugged
like she had no idea at all what language
your mother was speaking or what in the world she wanted,
ordering your mother to move, to stop blocking the other customers,
which made your pregnant, lonely mother turn
red and leave. She never tried again to ask
an American for chocolate. Such a luxury anyway,
she told herself. Not really something she couldn't
live without like the Americans she calls *shocoladniks.*
She laughs when she says they can't live without their candy bars.
Their cakes and pies. *Not like us Europeans.*
(She doesn't like to say she's from Poland.)
For us, chocolate is a luxury, not a necessity.
She doesn't say, but you know she's thinking about
the ones that were killed who can't eat chocolate anymore.
So why should she be so lucky.

When you go to a store together or she has to make a call
from the black telephone on the kitchen wall,
she asks you to speak for her. You know you shouldn't mind.
You should want to help your mother whose accent most people,
except for other *greena*, can't understand when she

tries to speak English. Your parents act almost proud
when you speak and Americans understand. Not only
can you say the words, you spell them right in English.
So you fill in all the blanks that need answers.
The papers for school. At the doctor's office.
The library. The bank. When your mother needs
a new driver's license.

How your parents write words in English is different
from the way Americans do. People wrinkle their noses,
act like they're staring at a puzzle, like your parents
just scribbled instead of tried their best
to make the letters right. Some people hand back the paper.
Look at you like your parents are from a different planet,
don't belong in America.
You mother gets embarrassed. Your father, furious.
You get angry too.

Sometimes you think those strangers
are pretending not to understand so they can insult your parents,
show they are stupid. Not as good as regular Americans.
But just because a person can talk and write without an accent
doesn't mean they are better than people who
talk and write *with* accents. And just because someone
spells things right and pronounces V's and W's like
they make different sounds, and says tricky English words,
like *psychology* and *night* and *cough* right, doesn't mean
they are better than other people who can't.

You want to yell at all the people who act sorry
that you have parents who are *immigrants*—
a fancy American word for *refugees,* which is
what your parents and their friends call themselves in English.

Refugees. Mostly they say they are *greena*
like it wasn't an insult even though you think it is.
But you don't tell them.

Another secret you don't tell is that you wish your parents
would never ask you again to talk for them.
In stores. On the phone. Or anywhere.
You are the kid and they are the parents.
You don't like acting smarter than them.
They might be proud for a few seconds in front of Americans
because their child can talk without an accent. Because
she was born here in America.

But they always remind you later that you
aren't smarter than them. Especially when you talk back.
When you make a face at the boiled spinach. Don't want to
go to birthday parties. Want to be alone. Or
if there's something else you want to decide for yourself.
Your mother yells that she is the boss of you.
Not the other way around. *Just because you talk English better*
doesn't mean for a minute that you know better than we do
what's best for you.
You hate when she says that, even though you're not allowed to hate.
You don't want her to be the boss of you.
And you don't want to be the boss of her.

Russell throws spitballs in third grade when Mrs. Cadave's back is turned.
Russell is fearless. *Impossible to control*, Mrs. Cadave says. Not like you.
Before being sent to sit in the hallway then to the principal's office
where he always winds up, Russell has to drag his chair
to the front of the class. So Mrs. Cadave can keep her eye on him
while she writes on the blackboard. Russell winks at you from up there
when he thinks she isn't looking and even if she is. You are the outcasts.
Him so daringly bad. You quiet as dust. Praying to be invisible because
it's so dangerous to be seen by Mrs. Cadave.

Maybe if you get quiet enough, she will forget about you. If only
you could be quiet enough. But you can't be. Well, *they* won't be.
Books dropping. Pencils snapping in half. Desktops slamming.
Lunchboxes rattling. It always works when they do those things.
Mrs. Cadave at the blackboard whips around. Points. *Little Jew*,
she accuses, commanding you to write 100 or 300 or 500 times,
depending how loud and startling the noise, the sentence that always
starts *I will not disturb the class by* ... and ends with the crime: *shutting my
lunchbox ... dropping my book ... snapping my pencil ... clearing my throat.*

Throwing a spitball. The one time she blames you for spitballs, Russell
shouts, *I did it. Not her. Don't blame her.* But Mrs. Cadave keeps on.
And they keep on too, holding their noses, saying *PU the Jew* every
single day soon as you open your lunchbox, even when you don't have
a sardine sandwich. Except for Russell. He never holds his nose
like you stink. Never. His jaw tight, he just chews more paper
into spitballs. Until one Monday, he starts up with rubber bands,
shot as soon as Mrs. Cadave isn't looking. And even when she is.

The first is pink. With the smallest key you ever saw.
A tiny twist of a turn in its lock protects your secrets.
At night you tuck the small diary under your pillow
to keep it safe. To feel the one you write to close to you.

You write *Dear Diary* at first. Then *Dear HaShem*.
The coziest name for God you know, not one of God's names
in your prayerbook with the blue cover or in the Torah.
More private. Like when your mother whispers *Nunya*
to your father. But not exactly like that, because God is God.

HaShem means The Name. Soon as you write it, it feels like
HaShem might hear you even though he's so busy
with children who need him more, children with no parents,
children starving in Africa, children in hospitals or
in just-crashed cars. You agree that God should go to them
first. You write that in your diary. That you want him
to go to who needs him the most. You know he might
always be busy. But you write him anyway for when maybe
God will have time to read what you wrote.
Dear HaShem is how you start every time.
Right away you feel not so alone. You wonder if maybe
it's really true that God can be in lots of places at once.

How happy you sometimes feel is the first big secret
you tell *HaShem*. Then you start to tell about the sad things.
You try not to complain. You know your problems are
nothing compared to real problems.

After the pink diary comes a shiny, black patent leather one.
Another tiny key. With more secrets to guard, you put

your locked diary in the new red vinyl treasure box you
get at the Elmer 5 & 10. It has its own key, so now
your diary is double locked. You don't want anyone,
especially your mother, to see the forbidden word.
Hate. You say it about your mother in your diary.
A huge sin against Number Five of the Ten Commandments.
Thou Shalt Honor Thy Father and Thy Mother.
You don't believe children should
have to honor their parents if their mothers and their fathers
don't honor them.

You used to believe that parents know everything
in their children's minds like your parents say they do.
Until that day you came back with chewing gum stuck
to your scalp that Donna Fagliarini told someone to put there.
When your mother asked how it got there, you told her
By mistake. I leaned my head back against a seat
that had gum on it. On the school bus.
An accident, too, you explained,
when your ponytail got set on fire.
Another one of Donna Fagliarini's ideas that she
bossed other kids to do.

When your mother didn't sink in her chair and
go back to Poland, but just was really annoyed while she
tried to pull the gum out and to cut off the burned ends,
you figured out that maybe parents
don't really know everything.

You tested it later just to be sure, thinking mean thoughts
when your mother's back was turned.
Your breasts look like mushy grapefruits.
You shouldn't light the candles with just your panties on.
You have stinky breath.

She didn't even turn around from washing dishes.
Didn't holler. No spanking.
That was when you figured out
your mind can be even more secret than your diary.
No one can open it.

You keep telling your diary things anyway. Things you
can't tell your mother because if you did
she would just suffer more. Like about Mrs. Cadave
and what happens in third grade.

What a huge surprise you never expected when one night after supper
your mother says, *I have an Announcement.*
She takes off her apron.
Asks everyone to sit down and listen, even your father.
Standing at the head of the table, she says:
In this house no one should ever read another person's diary.
She looks at you and with a kinder than regular voice, says
Ehni, you should not ever have to lock your diary. Or hide it.
In this house, she repeats louder now.
No one should have to worry that somebody else
will read their diary. The *no one* is you, the only one
in the whole family who has a diary.
You can hardly believe your ears.
There are tears in her eyes. You get tears in yours.

You wonder for the first time if maybe she had a diary
when she was a girl. If when her mother told her to leave,
to run away and save her life, if maybe
she left her diary hidden in the small house
that her mother, her brothers, and her little sister would
soon be forced to leave behind when they were rounded up.
Marched away.

In bed you tell Kathy that your mother's announcement
was a miracle.
You lock your diary anyway for a while
until you lose the tiny key
and decide
maybe it's safe
to trust her.

I.

You hear Mrs. Cadave walk down the row between desks.
She is coming toward you. You hold your breath.
Don't look up. Wish hard that by magic you would disappear.
But you never do. Quick you close your lunchbox. Keep
quiet. Out the corner of your eye you see her gray skirt,
hope she will walk past, leave you alone, not make fun.

She stops right next to you.
Thousands of wild butterflies trapped in your belly
scream without making a sound, too scared to be heard.
You are trapped like them. But out here in third grade.

Open your lunchbox, little Jew, Mrs. Cadave orders.
You know right away she saw it. The flat matzo sandwich
wrapped in aluminum foil. *Show the class what you have today.*

You don't want to obey but have to. You lift the lunchbox lid
slight as you can, slide out the matzo you brought because
it's Passover and a sin to eat bread. Between two long pieces
that remind you of chicken coop number 4's flat roof
are squished sardines, cream cheese, a smashed leaky slice
of tomato. You don't unwrap your matzo sandwich.
If peanut butter was gluing the matzo pieces together
that would be better. But no matter how much you beg for
peanut butter and jelly, your mother always says no.
You decided back in second grade not to tell about
how they yell *PU the Jew* even when you don't
have something stinky in your lunchbox, which is never.
Today it's not just the smell. It's also the shape of
what Mrs. Cadave calls your *Jew cracker sandwich.*

She orders you to unwrap it. *Now go to the front of the class,*
Little Jew. Show everyone your Jew cracker.
She's smiling like this is a fun Show and Tell. But it's not.
You don't get up.
She repeats, *Little Jew,* angrier now, *I said go to the front of the class!*
Her voice has poison in it.
You stand up. You have no choice.
Don't forget your cracker sandwich.

Looking down, you walk slow to the front of the room,
hear everyone laugh, start to sing *PU* even before
you hold up the matzo, extra careful to keep it flat
so no cream cheese, squished tomato, or worst of all
a piece of sardine will slide out and make everyone laugh harder.
Tell the class about your cracker sandwich, Mrs. Cadave bosses.

You know nobody wants to learn about Passover.
You whisper. *This is called matzo.* You hope Mrs. Cadave will
let you sit down now. Not because you're hungry. You aren't
one bit hungry. It's hard to eat things covered with *PU.*
You take one step toward the row where your desk is.
Stay there, little Jew. She starts walking toward you,
toward your stupid matzo sandwich that you wish you could
just throw in the garbage, wish you never brought in the first place.

Mrs. Cadave comes closer, a slice of white bread in her hand.
The kind of bread Americans eat, the same kind the aproned
friendly mother on TV makes sandwiches with for Wally and Beaver.
So different from your family's bread. A black pumpernickel loaf
that has to be cut with a special bread knife. And rye, with seeds
like tiny commas.

Mrs. Cadave stretches out her arm so the bread touches your lips.
Eat bread, little Jew. Let's see you eat the bread.

You can't eat bread on Passover. It's a sin. *You'll die.*
The butterflies go crazy in your belly. All of a sudden
you need to make number two really bad. But you
have to hold everything in, especially the tears crowding together
in your eyes. Eating bread on Passover is one of the worst sins
a person can ever do. You will be dead in a second.
Maybe Mrs. Cadave knows and that's why she says to do it.
So you will be dead in third grade. She will finally be
rid of you. They all will. You would like to be rid of third grade too.
But not this way, not because of a sin.

She moves the bread back and forth under your nose.
For a second, you imagine biting her hand. But you don't.
You also don't bite the bread. Because it's a sin and
because you're holding your matzo sandwich with both hands.
You press your lips together hard.

Open your mouth, she orders.
And even though you know you shouldn't,
you do. Mrs. Cadave pushes the bread in.
You let go the matzo. Wait for lightning to come
straight down into you.

The lightning doesn't come.

Swallow it now, the monster yells.
You feel like a rag doll with wobbly legs.
The salty tears in your mouth big as a lake.
With mushy white bread floating in it. Maybe
if you just swallow the bread, she will let you sit back down

until the bell rings and it's time for everyone to line up in rows
and leave. You try to chew.
More tears roll down into your mouth.
The bread turns into a lump that won't go down.
No matter how much you chew and try to swallow,
it won't go down.
Your throat is a gate the lump can't pass through.

Swallow it! the teacher repeats.
You are pretty sure she will hit you if you don't.
Please help me swallow, you beg God in your mind.
Please, even if it makes me die.
You wonder if the lightning is waiting
for the minute the bread is all the way inside your belly.
All of a sudden, the lump goes down.
Still no lightning.

Then you know.
The lightning must be striking your parents!
You aren't being punished for this terrible sin. They are.
Your little sister, too. Everything on the farm will be black ashes
when you get home. Nothing will be left because of *your* sin.
You close your wet eyes, picture a blinding bolt shooting
straight down from the sky. An arrow of light into your father's head,
your mother's, and little sister's.
Into the house. All the coops with all the chickens in them burning.
Kathy and Lucky gone too.
The swing by the willow and the willow.

II.

On the bus ride home, you prepare your brother.
Whisper so no one else will hear. *The farm won't be there.*
Mommy and daddy will be gone. When he asks you *Why?*

you say, *Because I ate bread. Mrs. Cadave made me eat bread.*
I will take care of you from now on.
You don't tell him how much you wish you were the dead one.
You don't want him to be afraid. After all, you're the big sister.
It's your job to take care of him now.

The house is still there when you get back from the bus stop.
The coops. The chicken hospital up on cinderblocks.
All the rest. You don't understand.

In the kitchen, you realize your mother doesn't know what happened.
If she did, her shoulders would be up that way they get,
her eyes all red. She'd be slumped in a kitchen chair,
wanting to be dead with the other dead ones.
Or she would be screaming.
But she just asks *how was your day?* Not listening for an answer.
You never tell the truth anyway.
Okay, you say.
Your brother, on his way to change out of his school clothes
probably thinks your warning was just a joke
so you could get to boss him more.

That night, you wait for the lightning while everyone
is sleeping. Fire in the middle of the night
to burn up the whole family.
But it doesn't come.

III.
The bellyaches that start the next morning hurt so much
you stay a long time on the toilet, bent over, crying.
You never had a bellyache this strong. Like a fist
inside you squeezing tight that won't let go.

You can't go to school this way, your mother says,
kneeling by the toilet, her face like she can feel
the hurting. You decide to try harder to keep secret
how much it hurts,
not to give her more pain.

The bellyaches come every morning after that.
The whole time everyone is eating breakfast, you
sit on the toilet, holding your belly, trying not to cry
as loud as the hurt makes you want to cry.
It doesn't stop in time for you to go to the bus stop.
So your daddy walks there with Marty.
Waits with him for the yellow bus.
Walks back home.

You are so surprised when right after
your daddy gets back, all of a sudden
the hurting stops. Just disappears.
You sit up straight, your regular self.
Ready to play outside.

After a bunch more days of bellyaches
that go away after the school bus comes,
your mother says it's time
to check your belly.

I.

Dr. Falheimer presses on your belly, which doesn't hurt like when you're
bent over the toilet, but you wish he wasn't doing it anyway.
After he's done checking, he asks your mother if
it's okay for him to talk with you. Alone. Just him and you without her.
Yes, doctor, she answers.
Goes out into the waiting room.
You are alone with Dr. Falheimer, the first time ever. He clears his throat.
I want to ask you some questions, Anne.
You wonder why his questions need to be secret from your mother.
Did anybody do something to you, something you didn't like?
You shake your head no, right away. But it's not enough
to make him stop. *Did someone hurt you, make you feel uncomfortable?*

Inside your belly, the butterflies are waking up, starting to fly around.
You can feel their flapping wings. *No,* you say, trying to
look like you are not telling a lie. *Nobody did anything.*
This is your first big out loud lie to a grown-up.
Except for lying to your parents by leaving things out.
This is different. A lie straight to someone's face.
But you *can't* tell the truth.
If you do and your parents find out, they will die or want to die.
They will think the Nazis are coming or here already.
Are you sure, Anne? Yes, you say, looking straight into his eyes
to prove you are telling the truth. *Nobody did anything,* you say again.
The butterflies want to scream but stay quiet as if they had
hands over their butterfly mouths. For just a second you want
to find a way to tell him. To tell him all about it. How Mrs. Cadave
made you eat bread. How she is *always* doing things that feel awful.
About the children always calling you a Devil. But you can't.
He would tell your parents. And it would all just be worse.

II.

At supper, your mother tells your daddy, *Dr. Falheimer asked Ehni*
if something happened. She told him nothing did.
You aren't surprised that Dr. Falheimer didn't keep a secret.
But something did happen, your brother blurts out. *Mrs. Cadave*
made Annie eat bread. On Passover. On the school bus she told me
you were going to be dead, that the farm would be all burned up.
So she would have to take care of me. You shoot him a look
you wish could strike him dead or at least freeze his mouth.
After the lightning didn't come for more than a week,
you told him to keep everything you said a secret. It's too late now.

Both your parents look at you. *Is that true, Ehni?* your mother asks.
Before you answer, she collapses into a chair with that look she gets
when she's seeing Nazis kill her mother, her brothers, her cousin.
Your daddy bangs his fist on the table.
Choleira! he shouts. *I'll teach them.*

III.

The bellyaches stop coming. The walks to the bus stop start again.
And the rides to school when the kids search for your devil horns.
You write on the blackboards *I am sorry for disturbing the class.*
For things the other kids do. When it's 500 times, you hold
one arm up with the other hand. Hide that you are crying.

IV.

You're surprised that neither of your parents talk again
about you eating bread on Passover. You're not sure why.
But are glad they don't. Then one night at supper,
your daddy says he went to Jacksonville School to tell the principal
what happened. Asked him to control his teacher.

Told him that what happened should never happen again.
Your daddy looks at your mother. *Do you know what he answered me?!*
What he said to me?! That choleira told me: Who ever said we wanted
you people here? Hitler should have finished you all off.

Your mother falls into a chair. Is having trouble breathing.
I took him by his tie, your daddy goes on. He grabs the air to
show how he pulled the principal's tie.
You get afraid your daddy choked the principal.
Wonder what will happen now to all of you.
He goes on, ignoring that your mother might die listening to this.
I told him: If that teacher of yours ever does anything like that again
to my child, I will kill you. And I mean it.

V.
Your daddy doesn't kill the principal of Jacksonville School because
you get better at secrets. You don't ever let them know what Mrs. Cadave
keeps on doing in third grade, so he won't come to the school again.
You never trust your brother with another secret, of course. Just Kathy,
Lucky, and the willow. Mostly, you only think your secrets,
don't say them out loud just in case someone might hear.
Right after The War, your daddy beat up, maybe even killed Jews who
sold other Jews to the Nazis for *zlotys,* sugar, or coffee. You know
because of his nightmares when your mother tells him it's okay,
that God forgives him. So he can go back to sleep.
But if your daddy kills the principal of the school, even if he deserves it,
the police in America might come and kill your daddy.
Better to keep secret what Mrs. Cadave does and makes you do.
Better that your daddy believes he *taught those antisemites a lesson.*
That he protected you.

I see you waiting. Something you are good at.
It's easier some places than others. Like now.
This summer night under a blue-black satin sky.
You sing *Catch a Falling Star.*

Catch a Falling Star and Put in your Pocket
Never Let it Fade Away
Catch a Falling Star and Put it in your Pocket
Save It for a Rainy Day

Over and over.
Because those are the only words
you know to the song. Your favorite.
Perry Como sings it with a voice smooth as darkness.
Like he believes there are beautiful stars you can catch
if you watch carefully, wait for them to fall. You believe it too
even though you wouldn't tell your parents you do.
They think almost all good things are
too good to be true. To catch a star and keep it in your pocket
would definitely be a too-good-to-be-true thing.

Catch a Falling Star and Put in your Pocket
Never Let it Fade Away
You close your hand in the pocket of your shorts
around a star you pretend fell that you caught and put there.
Your other hand palm up to the night sky. Ready.

You walk farther from the house where the darkness
is darker and they won't hear you sing loud.
Catch a Falling Star and Put in your Pocket

Save It for a Rainy Day. You sing it like Perry Como does.
Happy and free.

After a while you think maybe it's okay if you don't
ever catch
a real star.
That it's enough to look up at them sparkling
like God was winking at you with a whole lot of eyes
at once.

You lie down in the grass. Look up.
At first it's hard to keep singing. The huge sky above
makes you quiet.

Then you start. Whisper now instead of loud.
Catch a Falling Star and Put in your Pocket
Never let it fade away   Never
Let it
Fade
Away
When you feel a tear of happiness roll from your eye,
you touch it with your fingertip, imagine
it's a star.

He lives next door.
Not in a house. In a falling down shack
just past the wild blueberries tangled with prickers.
You hear him easier than see him.
But sometimes when there aren't so many leaves on the trees
you see him too.

He's kind of caved in like his shack.
He stumbles around and falls down a lot.
Yells curse words. Throws beer cans.
Sometimes he throws them in the air and tries to
shoot them, another reason for you to
be careful and make Marty and Shelly be careful too.
Blueberry Man has a gun.

Your parents say to ignore him like they say
about so many things you can't ignore.

Instead, you check on him a lot.
In sneaky ways. Down on your knees.
Peeking through the blueberries on your belly
so he won't see you watching.

You're relieved he never
crashes through the blueberries by accident
because he's drunk or on purpose because he's mad.
His beer cans never land in the field you watch from.
His gun doesn't point toward the blueberries you squat behind.
If he ever does point that way, you hope he will fall down
before shooting.

Then something happens.
Chickens start disappearing from the coops.

No one is stealing my chickens, your daddy hollers
one suppertime. *Do they think I'm a fool?*

Your daddy gets a gun from you don't know where.
He waits until the full moon shines its light over the farm.
Says he's going to stay up all night to wait for the thief.
Your mother cries.
Begs him not to go out.
Didn't we lose enough?

He tells her not to worry.
He thinks it's only Blueberry Man—not what your daddy
calls him, but you know that's who he means when he says,
The shikkur next door who can't even stand up straight.

Your daddy's plan is to wait outside, to
hide in the shadows.

You wait too. In your bed.
Hear the shot. Squeeze Kathy tight.
Wait for more shots.
There isn't another.

You hear your daddy come in extra quiet.
Hear him go into the small bedroom, whisper to your mother.
But you can't hear what.
You wonder if Blueberry Man is dead now,
think he kind of deserved it
but feel sorry for him at the same time.

In the morning your daddy says
he shot up into the sky. Just to scare him.
Says Blueberry Man froze
like an animal when light shines on it.
He dropped the chickens. Two of them,
One under each arm. Still alive.

Your daddy laughs. *Such a daring thief*
on his knees begging me that I should only not kill him.
GO! I told him.
It took him longer than it took the chickens
to find his legs
and run.

Not every Friday before sundown, but most, your daddy
calls the three of you into the kitchen. Before the candles are lit.
Because then is *the best time to give tzedakah*, he says.
He lifts the *pushka* off its nail, the small blue, partly rusted, tin box
with a white menorah on it and Hebrew letters. He shakes it.
You can tell it's getting pretty full. *Maybe a little more room left*,
he says. Puts it back on its nail.

The *pushka* is in the kitchen all the time.
But *Shabbos* is when you pay more attention to it and to the children
far away who the money in the *pushka* will buy food and clothes for.

You line up. You the oldest, first in line to put the nickels, dimes, and
quarters into the small slot that you pretend is the *pushka*'s mouth,
always open for coins, always wanting more so its belly can get full.
Your daddy gives you a handful, mostly brown pennies, some silver coins.
You are just tall enough now to reach the mouth without standing
on a chair, the way your little sister will when it's her turn.
You like to go slow, not hurry like your brother to stuff coins in
fast as he can. You put them in one by one by one. Slower than
your daddy would. This, one of the only times he doesn't try to change
how you do things different than him.

His eyes behind his glasses get shiny with tears on the days
you give *tzedakah*. No matter how little your family has, he says,
*no matter how bad making a living is on the farm, if we have
enough for food, a roof over our heads, a few dollars for clothes,
we have to share the rest with people who don't have enough.*

The *pushka* full now, no more coins fitting in,
your daddy brings the tin box to the kitchen table,

opens the bottom. You three stand around him
while the jangly coins rush out like a waterfall.
You chase the ones that roll off the Formica table,
so not a single one for the children is lost by mistake.

He makes little piles of coins. You help him count them,
each pile two times. Then he writes a *check*, a piece of paper
that tells exactly what the quarters, nickels, and dimes add up to.
He signs it with his name, starting with a big fancy letter *A*
for Arnold and a big swirly *T* for the front of Tuzman.
Then he gets one of the blue, onionskin *Aerogrammes*
he uses for letters to his brother Avrom in Israel.
He folds the aerogramme around the check. Lets you lick it shut.
You don't say that you can't wait to someday
write letters on magic paper made of blue onions.

He writes the address in Hebrew letters. Reads it out loud.
The name of an orphanage in Jerusalem.

You didn't know at first but now you do that an orphanage
is a place children live who don't have mothers or fathers.
Orphans are people whose mothers and fathers got killed.
Like your parents. They are orphans. Which they never forget,
not even for a second. That is why there are always wet spots on the
aerogramme that smear the ink. The spots are your daddy's tears.

Your father is a softy, your mother says with a smile,
coming closer to the table from the stove.
She strokes the top of your daddy's head. Leans over and kisses him
on his forehead and cheeks. This is the opposite of normal
when she is the one crying mixed with screaming
and your daddy has to try to bring her back from The War.
Back to the farm, to him, and the three of you.

But the nights of giving *tzedakah* when your daddy's
eyes fill with tears that smear the address, those Fridays
just before she lights the Sabbath candles, your mother
becomes the strong one, proud of him for not being strong.

I see you on a bench at the edge of the boardwalk,
your back to the clacking heels, rumble of rolling chairs,
the bazillion different voices.
Peanuts for sale! Peanuts!
Get your tickets to the Steel Pier!
Cotton candy here! Balloons! Balloons!
Don't run ahead—you'll get lost!
Check out our beach toy bonanza!
The best arcade in Atlantic City—three throws for a dime!
Go for the jackpot!

You face the ocean. Cannot see it in the night. Can just hear it.
Faint at first, as if you were imagining it there.
You push your face forward. Close your eyes.
Listen harder.

You hear the waves rush in like they
love the shore, left alone now. Empty of crowds.

You lean deeper into the dark.
A kind breeze meets you.
The ocean with no end. The night. Your face.
All there is.

The steady whoosh of the waves makes you cry. With longing
to be closer to the ocean than even when swimming in it,
buoyed, skin coated with salt. Diving beneath its surface.
Closer even than that.
You want what separation there is
between you and the ocean
to be gone.
No longer to be a separate girl on a bench.

You hear your name called.

Your parents back from buying peanuts in paper cones.

Your father laughing. *Why are you looking where there's nothing to see?*

Turn around. Join the human race, my daughter.

You smell the peanuts.

Don't want to open your eyes, to be pulled from the dark.

Away from the ocean's summons. With no choice but to leave

this moment when there is nothing else

but the ocean, the deep night, and you.

May the Lord bless you

 Your father swings the live chicken over your heads.

and keep you.

 Your mother watching,

 always reminded of her father.

May the Lord make his countenance shine upon you

 You imagine God's face,

 thinking it a sin to wish to see God.

and be gracious unto you.

 How can a chicken take your sins?

May the Lord lift his countenance toward you

 What does God really want?

and give you peace.

 Your father is crying by the end, promising you

 when he breaks its neck, the chicken

 will feel almost nothing.

Yom Kippur. The Day of Atonement.
When it is finally decided Who Shall Die by Fire.
And Who by Stoning.
Who by Drowning. And Who by Snakes.
Who by Thirst. And Who by Earthquake.

And who shall die by all the rest.

You imagine that Book of Life so heavy
it should be falling down right now from the sky
through the flimsy clouds. Right out of God's hands
through the roof of the Elmer shul, the little wooden house of prayer
on this Day of Awe, not sure exactly what *Awe* should feel like.

If someone has to *perish,* you know it should be you.
So you think fast to God in your head
while the people around you mumble their prayers.
You hurry your pleas, so they'll get there before
God starts with whatever pen he uses, black ink probably,
to inscribe The Decrees. *Please don't make my parents suffer more.*
They don't deserve any Decree except Life.
You picture the slimy snakes curled up at the bottom of the cesspool,
close your eyes tight and continue.
I'll even die in a snake pit if it means saving them.

You have the feeling maybe you aren't supposed to be
making deals with God. Then you remember
the Torah is full of them.
For ten righteous ones, I will save an entire village,
God said then bargained down,
promising to do it for just one righteous man.

And what about a lamb on an altar
traded for a son?

You decide that compared to snakes,
the other Decrees aren't so bad.
You hope God will be *merciful* if it's wrong
to make deals. It is after all The Season of Forgiveness.
God would probably forgive anyone who is really sorry.

Your parents probably won't pray for themselves.
They believe they've been saved too many times.
If they do dare ask to be kept alive it will be because
their children need them.
If the dead can pray, then your dead grandmothers
and dead grandfathers are all pleading at God's elbow
that their daughter Esther and their son Aharon (his real name)
be spared.

The hour of *Ne'ilah* comes. The closing prayers
just before the heavy sun sets on each Jew's destiny.
A last-minute chance to *avert judgment* before
The Book of Life is sealed. *You keep praying*
hard and loud as you can without moving or making a sound.
When *Ne'ilah* is finished, there's nothing left for you to do
but listen for The Book to close.

In the morning, you ride your bike fast into the wind,
wondering if you did enough to protect your parents.
To avert The Severe Decrees.

They are going to New York,
taking Shelly. If you and Marty need anything,
you should ask Jasper who is helping on the farm.
Your mother says she will bring back *a souvenir,*
which means a gift from a place someone visits.
A very special surprise! she promises.

They come back late. Think you're asleep.
But you're not.

The next morning after breakfast, your mother tells you to
close your eyes and put out your hand. Right away you feel
selfish because you want the souvenir to be bigger than
what fits in one hand. You put out both hands just in case.

She puts something into one of them.
Okay! Open your eyes! Her voice sounds excited.
Like the souvenir must be extra special.
You open your eyes. Look down and see.

A change purse.
It's a small see-through-plastic
change purse. A zipper on top.
A tiny green Statue of Liberty design on it.

This is it? The souvenir? you think but don't say.

But it's too late.
She sees your *sour look* and starts
turning into her monster self.
You wish you could take it back. Your look.

The not being excited about what she gave you.
But you can't.

She grabs the change purse, scratching you by accident.
Two beads of blood in your palm
where the souvenir was.

What? It's not a nice enough gift for you?
You think money grows on trees? Her voice climbs.
I have news for you. We work like dogs. I take one day
away from this fahshthinkenna farm and you give me a sour look?
I'll show you a beautiful souvenir.

She gets the big scissors out of a drawer near the sink.
You call out fast *I'm sorry. I didn't mean it. It's a very nice*
change purse. But it's too late. She isn't listening.
If she can hear you, she isn't paying attention.
She's too busy stabbing the change purse with the scissors.
Maybe if you told her *I really love it.*
But that would be lying. You don't love it at all.
It's not true that you want a souvenir that costs a lot of money.
You just wish it was a thing
you liked more.

She starts cutting. Yells that she's going to
teach you a lesson you will never forget.
Are you watching? This is what happens to
a selfish little girl who isn't satisfied with what she gets.

You think she's done when the change purse is cut into
four pieces of itself. But she cuts those pieces smaller
and smaller until there are tiny bits of plastic on the floor
like the change purse is dead now and you
just watched her kill it.

Now are you happy? she asks.
Even though she knows you're not.

She drops the scissors as if all of a sudden
they are too heavy to hold.
Let this be a lesson, my daughter. Her voice now
more sad than mad.

After she leaves the kitchen, you kneel.
Gather up the pieces so she won't have to.

I see you sitting under a wide-skirted pine, the third in the row
by the chicken hospital. A square shed up on cinderblocks
where sick chickens cluck different than the ones in the coops.
Your black patent leather diary is open on your lap. You love
feeling hidden. As if they don't know where you are, don't even
have a clue. As if you are actually invisible and they with no way
to reach you. Not with eyes or their voices. You so close
but impossibly far.

That is how you always feel. Too close and so far. Without the
words to explain how different from them you are. As if
the joke they tell, laughing in the kitchen about the milkman
a joke you do not really understand, was not a joke at all.
The milkman brought her.

You try to imagine how it was. You a tiny baby left in
the metal box with the four glass milk bottles or
not *in* the box but next to it, wrapped in blankets.
Your parents feeling sorry for a lonesome baby
who they could see was so different from them.
A *button nose*, not a Jewish one, *eyes like she's Chinese.*
But they keep you.

You wish hard now that when the milkman came back,
he would have found you still outside and *right then,*
the kind milkman would have decided to take you back.
To find a family that's a better match, one where
the mother is not always thinking about a War.
Maybe a family with parents who love books
or who know how to relax a little without schnapps
on a sofa not wrapped in plastic.

But it's too late now you suppose from under your pine,
hearing the screen door slam behind her, to have a different mother.
Not the one hollering your name now while you pretend
not to hear her, wondering how long you can ignore her
before she gets angrier than she already is about how you
would always rather write in your diary or read books
than play with your sister or pack eggs or learn to cook.
How did I raise such a selfish little girl? she says often.
But you know that she thinks it's *your* fault not hers
that you are how you are.
She never blames the milkman. Even though
he's the one who brought you.

Some you don't remember.
Like when you threw hay on top of your baby brother who was
sound asleep in the chicken feed carrier that looks like a swinging bathtub
just inside the door to chicken coop number 4
whose roof Hurricane Hazel lifted off like it was just a big flat hat
then dropped in a pile of manure in front of chicken coop number 6.

Hazel came after Marty wasn't a baby anymore. But when he was,
not only did you try to bury him
while your parents were in coop number 4 collecting eggs,
you also threw your father's ice skates
right over the bars into Marty's crib while he was in it.
After that you pushed a chair close to the crib, climbed in,
and sat on top of Marty's head—on a pillow you threw in first.

They stopped leaving you alone with him.
Because of how dangerous you were. Three years old.
How in the world you figured out to do such things
we have no idea, your parents still say.
Your mother called Dr. Falheimer to see if something
was wrong with you. *Sibling Rivalry,* he told her, words
very hard to pronounce. She should get a book, he said,
by a doctor: *The Common Sense Book of Baby and Child Care.*
She keeps it next to Amy Vanderbilt's *ETIQUETTE*. The two books
that teach her the right ways to be American and a mother. Books
your father never reads. When your mother says *This is what Dr. Spock*
thinks, your father just answers *Pissss-sigh-chology.* Says it slow.
Their American Pissss-sigh-chology. They can keep it.
He says it like it's all a big waste of time and *nobody*
is going to tell him what to do. Especially an American doctor

who doesn't believe in spanking which everyone knows
is the best, fastest way to teach children right from wrong.

A few of the things you get spanked for:
When you hold your nose around your little sister.
When you make a face the minute your mother
sets your plate down with boiled spinach on it or peas, or boiled carrots.
When you talk back because you don't agree with your mother,
which she never did when *her* mother was alive.
When you say you hate your brother or sister. That gets the worst
spanking of all. Because there is a rule in your house:
Nobody should hate or even feel hate under this roof.
Hate is a curse word in this family, your mother says.
Except for hating the Nazis and Hitler, *his name should be erased.*
Because they are a different category. Not human beings.

You mostly get spanked for all the ways you are stubborn.
You being stubborn started before you could even talk,
your mother reminds you. When you were only one and a half
and they still lived in Brooklyn, you would hold your breath
and turn blue. Even pass out. You made it so hard for her,
she tells you often. She, a lonely refugee. A young mother
without a mother to guide her. She was afraid you might die.
Didn't know what to do, how to stop you. Until one day
someone told her *this is* a *temper tantrum.* Your mother should
just ignore you, let you hold your breath, turn blue, fall down—
until you learned you wouldn't get your way. That would put an end to it.
One day you did it on East New York Avenue where a whole lot of
people were passing. They started hollering at her to do something.
To rescue her child. She looked down, couldn't tell them in English that
this was just your bad temper. That she was *trying to get it out of you*
for once and for all. You know she doesn't think she ever
did get it out of you. Your stubbornness. Your *strong will.*

Your father does the spanking. He uses the Kill Belt.
You and Marty named it that, the belt that hangs on a hook
on the other side of the door that leads up to the attic. The belt
that is only for spanking not for your daddy's pants.
But you and Marty have to pull your pants down. Sometimes even your
underpants have to get pulled down a little, so you will feel it on your skin
and be sorry. You lean across his knees, your head hanging on one side,
your legs on the other, kind of like you're folded over his big knee.
He asks *Are you ready*? Raises his arm high, holding the belt up.
Counts: *1 2 3*. Then brings it down.
Usually, you know how many times it will be depending on
how bad what you did was. 4 or 5 times usually. For talking back,
maybe 6 or 7. You always squeeze your eyes shut. Try to be
strong and not too sorry. That way it won't hurt so much.

Sometimes you sneak a look at your father after the spanking is done,
see his eyes red from tears. He says with a quiet voice,
You know I love you, ketsella. I just want to make sure
you grow up the right way.

He's wrong about spanking being a help. The opposite.
But you don't say so or they will call it your stubbornness
and try to find more ways to get it out of you.

Like Huckleberry Finn when he ran away from home,
you tie a hanky to a stick (a branch you've been hiding).
Inside your hanky satchel is:
A banana. A sharpened yellow pencil
with its eraser not used up. A piece of paper.
Your sweater doesn't fit no matter how you scrunch it,
so you tie its arms around your shoulders,
kind of like it's hugging you.

You put your goodbye note under
a saltshaker on the kitchen table,
You wrote it with their ballpoint pen on a thick smooth paper napkin.
Even if it does waste a napkin, it will be the last one.

> *I am running away from home.*
> *I know you will be happier without me part of this family*
> *because you ~~don't love me~~ I don't belong here.*
> *from Annie*

You've been waiting for the right time. Now it's here.
Your mother just left with Shelly to Dr. Falheimer's office.
Marty said he wanted to go too. You said, *No thank you.*
Your father is with Jasper in coop number 6 fixing a broken window.
There's no one to stop you or tell on you when you sneak out the door
with your satchel.
You didn't think it would be this easy. Thought it would take
more sneaking.
The screen door slams behind you for the last time.

You walk fast to kiss the willow goodbye,
Lucky isn't around. You're kind of glad.

This way, she won't follow you,
barking hints about where you are.
You've been hugging Lucky goodbye every day. Just
in case, you didn't get to on the day of running away.
You walk fast by the cesspool
then past the cement marker that shows you're now
on a stranger's property. Being in someone else's woods
means you are getting far from the house with the family
that doesn't want you in it.

You stop. Go stand behind the fattest tree you can find
then peek to check if you can see the house. You can.
You try to guess if they can see you. Decide they can't.
Put your satchel down. Sit on the ground next to it. Untie the hanky.
Take out, peel, and eat the banana. Throw the peel far as you can.
Wonder what else to do before the time for dying.

Sunlight peeks through the leaves. You decide
it will be best to die before it gets dark. There's still time left.
Sweeping some leaves out of the way, you make a bald spot.
Write the letter *A* there with a sharp rock. Then the rest of your name.
A n n i e carved into the hard ground.
You poke a little hole over the *i* for its dot.

Three favorite things you didn't bring are Kathy, your diary,
and a book. You left them home on purpose.
You won't be writing in your diary anymore. And dead people
don't read books.
Not bringing Kathy was the hardest decision. You decided together
that it's best for *just you* to die. She doesn't have to die too.
They don't yell at her, don't hit her, don't not like her.
So Kathy can keep on living. You hope your sister will be kind to her,
treat her a little like you do. If Shelly isn't kind, you are pretty sure
Kathy will figure out a way to get away.

People say dolls can't run away. But you know they are real
and have powers.
Kathy understands why you want to run away from home. She agrees
that it's a good idea even though you will be apart
and will miss each other so much. You already miss her.
Neither of you knows if dead people can miss anyone.
You do know you won't miss your family. Even more true
is that they won't miss you.

You hear your mother call you. Hold your breath. Don't answer.
The screen door slams when she goes back inside. You don't move.
After it's quiet for a while, you stand up behind the fat tree.
check if anyone is walking around maybe looking for you.
Nobody.

You have to make number one. Pull down your shorts and panties.
Squat and pee. It soaks into the ground.
You push leaves over the wet with your Ked. Smile.
It doesn't matter anymore if your Keds, polished white as chalk,
get really dirty. You wore them today on purpose for running away.
You don't have to keep them clean anymore.

You take out the piece of paper and the pencil.
You brought them just in case you would have one last message.
You don't know what to write or who to write to.
You write *I*. Your pencil point pokes through the paper because
the ground is bumpy with tree roots.
You put the pencil back into the hanky satchel. Crumple up the paper.
Put it in the satchel too.
Decide you can just think a message if you have one.

Running away from home almost starts to get a little boring.

You hear your mother holler your name.

She says it two more times. Then she hollers, *It's time for supper.*

You stay as still as the fat tree you're leaning against.

Hear her holler, *You will be hungry, Ehni.*

You are a little hungry already.

Dead girls don't feel hungry, you are pretty sure.

Soon you will be a dead not-hungry girl.

It's getting chilly. You untie your sweater's arms and put in on.

You didn't bring a blanket because it was too big to carry and

anyway dead girls don't get cold.

When it starts to get a little darker in the woods, you decide

it's time to die.

You lie down on your back straight as you can be.

Like you're doing an upside-down dead girl's float

except with your arms at your side not over your head.

You get ready to die.

Say goodbye in your mind to Kathy and Lucky.

To your willow again, too.

You close your eyes. *Okay, I'm ready to die* you think to the sky.

Nothing happens.

You wonder if maybe part of how you die is that

you have to say it out loud.

You whisper, *I'm ready to die.*

Nothing.

You open your eyes, see the leaves looking down.

Say louder but not too loud,

I want to die because they will be happier without me.
You close your eyes again.
Wait.

Then you realize, sit up.
People need Nazis to die.
You can't just lie down and die. You need Nazis or
at least *one* Nazi to kill you so that you'll be dead.
But there aren't any Nazis here right now.
You don't know any other way to die. Maybe if you wish hard enough?
Maybe then you can die without a Nazi?

You will try, lying down again.
You squeeze your eyes shut super tight, tighter than you ever
squeezed them before. Until they almost hurt.
You wish for dying to happen.
It doesn't.

You stay lying on the ground for a long time.
Roll over. Stretch out like
in a real dead man's float except on hard ground.

When you wake up, the sun is lower behind the trees.
You wanted to die. Not have a stupid nap.
You stand up behind the fat tree, peek at the house.
With its lights on the house looks like it has eyes.
Eyes that are looking for you. Its lights would
shine the way home if you decide to go back and
be part of that family again.
You don't want to go back,
even though you're shivering and hungry. But if you can't die
what will you do in the woods?
It would be different if Kathy was with you. Or Lucky. Or your diary.

But you're all alone.
All alone and not knowing how to die.

You open the screen door being quiet as you can so
it won't squeak or slam when you close it behind you.
Take off your dirty Keds. Put them next to each other,
socks rolled up and stuffed in.
You open the kitchen door.
Look down as you walk through, waiting for your mother
to scream at you any minute. Your father
to already have the Kill Belt ready.

Nobody says anything. Not a word.

You peek enough to see your mother sitting at the kitchen table.
Like a quiet statue not her regular self.
Her breathing sounds like it's hard work to get enough air in.
You keep walking.
Through the whole kitchen without anyone doing anything.
A miracle.

You get into your bed without taking your clothes off,
leaves stuck to them. You pull the blankets
over you and Kathy. Hug her so tight that for a minute
she can't breathe. You know she doesn't mind—
so happy to be in your arms again.
You don't have to tell her anything. She knows.

Maybe when you figure out how a person can die without Nazis
you'll run away again.
For now, you wait for your parents
to come teach you a lesson.

She enters a lot quieter than usual in the dark .
You hold your breath. Wait for her anger to tear the
delicate quiet, to disturb the nest where you are hiding.
You pretend to be asleep. Peer through a slit of eye
to see her silhouette, the kitchen chair she carries,
sets down close to your bed.
She sits. Her knees touch the edge of your mattress.
So close you hear her breathing, labored from
chicken feathers and dust. She whispers your name.
Softer, kinder than usual.

It's Mary, she says next. *Pretend I'm a stranger,
not your mother.*
You can tell Mary anything. Mary can keep secrets.
I won't tell your mother, I promise.

You stay very very still. Hold your breath until
you can't anymore. Open both eyes, wonder if
she knows you are awake. *Will you talk to me?* she asks
*I think there are some things bothering you. Maybe you can
tell Mary.*

You wait for her to be more like herself. Loud. Sad.
So sad that nothing you do can ever make it better.
I am here to listen, she says. Like she isn't mad.
About anything. Like she could just wait there.
Like you are not doing anything wrong, even though
you always are. Even though you do almost everything wrong.

You tell her just a little about the teasing.
The searching for horns in your hair.
After you tell, you wait for her to scream.

But she doesn't. She just whispers,
Honey, tell me more. I am Mary.
I can listen.

She isn't at all like your mother. Doesn't break
like a fragile cup that
even when it's not dropped
shatters anyway.
Into sharp pieces. Pieces that cut.
Tonight there is nothing sharp. Not her voice.
Not her red fingernails that can scratch.
None of that now when she is *Mary*.

It's hard to believe she won't change back into herself.
But she stays not mean.
Doesn't yell about Hitler, the Nazis, cry about her parents.
Doesn't ask *Why am I alive? Why did I survive?*
She acts like it's okay for you to feel sad.
Doesn't say what you feel can't be compared to what she went through.
That you have no right to cry about anything
because what do you know about *real suffering?*

Mary wouldn't say it's wrong you cry in your bed every night,
don't want to go to school,
sometimes even wish you weren't Jewish. A huge sin
your regular mother would spank you for.
Mary is a stranger you wish was your real mother.

If she ever comes back another night to sit by you in the dark,
maybe you will trust her. Answer her questions.
Believe she can hear your secrets without them hurting her.
Maybe you would let her touch you.
Maybe she would rest her kind hand on the side of your face,
wet with hot tears.
Maybe it would feel good to have her hand there.

A dream come true, seeing those huge photographs on the four walls.
Children from all over the world. The beautiful colors of their skin.
The shapes of their eyes. Hearing their music on records.
Listening to them talk and sing in all their different languages.
How they laugh with their eyes in the same language as you
no matter where they are.
You never felt this way before with a bunch of children. Like you belong
even though they're strangers. But not really strangers
because it feels like you are all part of one family.

Your first time at the United Nations building is when you
all go to New York to visit Tanta Rae who doesn't come,
but packs tuna fish sandwiches to take because *You never know* she says.
You are too excited to eat anything after the tour that ends in the gift shop
with pictures of children from the whole wide world.

You don't dare try to tell your parents how it feels. Like you are
finally in a place you were waiting to be your whole life
without knowing how much you were waiting until you found it.
A place where all your wishes can come true. Because
these children are holding hands.
It doesn't matter how different they are. No one
is left out.

The next time will be at the World's Fair when you hear
It's a Small World After All. You'll cry for the whole ride,
your eyes so watery it will be hard to see the children dancing.
But you will hear their voices sing the same song
in all their different ways. Your heart will want to bust out of you
from being so happy to see them together wanting peace as much as

you do. Wanting there to be no wars. Wanting nobody to boss children,
to hurt them, to kill them. Wanting children everywhere to have
clothes to wear, food to eat, places to live, books to read.
Wanting them to be free.

You decide someday when you are a grown-up you will
work for UNICEF, will help children be free who aren't yet.
Will make sure they have the things they need and they deserve—
the biggest one of all, RESPECT.
Because with that one, you are pretty sure,
the rest will come.

I.

You decide to ride your bike past Terry's house.
You know you're not supposed to. But you never
give up on Terry maybe one day becoming
your friend, the only other girl around for miles
except for your sister who's too little to count.

You hear the hollering from down the road. So loud,
you stop before you get all the way there.
You dismount your bike-horse, walk her slow and quiet
into the bushes by the side of the road.
You stroke her handlebars gently. Tell her you'll be back.

Stooping low, you make your way through the bushes
until you hear the angry words clear. You see a woman
throw something off a porch, hollering while she does.
Words like the ones Terry yells at the bus stop.
She throws a can with every word. *Motherfucker,* she screams,
Tipping to the side when she throws, almost falling down.
Sonofabitch. Another can flies. *Little bastard.* Two cans,
one right behind the other. She grabs the railing for balance.
Goddambitch good for nothing rotten pieceashit.
Go to hell! Her spit drips when she says what you know are
curse words. Bad words. You don't know what a *bastard* is
or a *sonfabitch* or a *motherfucker.* Or the difference between
a little bastard and a regular sized one.
The woman's voice is scratchier, even angrier than your mother's
except maybe for when your mother says Hitler's name and
spits three times after to get it out of her mouth.

You stand up higher in the bushes to get a better peek
at the yelling woman. Stand up even taller when
she turns her back to the road where you are standing,
one of her hands holding tight to the broken porch railing.
You can see better now. White and red cans with fancy
letters. *Shlitz.* The same kind of beer that the *greena*
bring to A Lion's Beach. But these are bent cans like
somebody drank all the beer up then bent the cans to throw them away.
But not into the garbage—at someone.
Standing on tiptoe you see who.
It's Terry.

Terry is the one the wild woman with a torn apron
is throwing the cans at. Terry looks more like a scared cat
than a mean fourth grade girl who never ever looks afraid.
Not at the bus stop. Not when she's the boss of other kids,
orders them to smell you. Now Terry reminds you
of a turtle afraid to move one inch.
She doesn't holler back at the woman, doesn't say even a single word.
Terry ducks some of the cans. But not too much ducking
because the woman who you think is Terry's mother
gets even madder when Terry ducks. Curses louder.
Throws the cans faster.
Until she runs out of cans. Yells *you good for nothing*
rotten little bastard and stumbles backwards into the house.

Terry doesn't move.
You wonder if she's crying but you're too far away to see if
her eyes have tears in them or not. You never saw Terry cry.
You feel sad for her. A new feeling. You never felt sorry for Terry
before now. Not even a tiny bit. But you do now, a whole lot.
Your mother doesn't know these curse words or

throw beer cans at you. But she hollers like crazy too and
you hate when she does. Terry probably hates it too when
her mother hollers at her. Maybe now Terry
will want a friend. Maybe now she
needs a friend.

You tiptoe out of the bushes quiet as you can
so that her angry mother won't come back out.
No cars coming. None probably will.
You take a few small steps toward Terry.
Wave, just a little wave.

Terry is looking down, standing still. Like a sad statue.
If she wasn't held together by skin, you think she might break.
Like one of those fancy dolls in Tanta Rae's apartment whose
left arm and right hand broke off when she fell from a shelf.
It looks like both Terry's arms and her head might fall off,
the way they are just hanging there.
But instead of breaking into pieces, Terry looks up.
Sees you there.
You wave again to show her you want to be her friend.

She stands up taller like a humped-over cat who was
afraid for a second but is now ready to attack.
She narrows her eyes into slits. Spits on the ground.
Dirty Little Jew, get out of here! Get out right now!

But I-I want to be your friend, Terry doesn't come out
in more than a small whisper. Terry starts yelling louder.
Motherfucker little dirty Jew bastard. She grabs a can to throw at you.
Then more cans. Throws them faster and faster.
You step back so the cans won't reach you.
But you don't turn away. Don't leave.
The red-and-white cans fly through the air with her words,

some of the same ones Terry's mother yelled along with others
that she didn't. *Dirty Jew-devil. Rotten Jesus-killer.*
Drop dead. Why don't you just drop dead!

It's no use, you know. Terry won't be your friend.
Even if you were the only two girls stranded on an island together.
You should go get your bike-horse and ride home.
But you just keep looking at Terry instead, wishing hard
without saying it out loud that Terry would change her mind.

All of a sudden, you see something.
You squeeze your eyes shut then open them
to check if it's still there. *It is.*
A little flame in the center of Terry's chest.
You can see it. And somehow you know that it was
always there. You just couldn't see it until now.
Something let you see right *into* Terry.
A light inside her. Tiny, like the flame of a Chanukah candle.
You can't stop looking at it.
Even when one of the cans hits your leg, you
can't take your eyes off the light inside Terry.

Nothing can put out that light. You know.
No mean words or bent beer cans, not a hurricane.
Nothing can put out that light. You just know.
Because it's *inside* Terry.
It stays lit even when Terry is asleep, even when she's
being yelled at by her falling-down mother.
Even when Terry spits and pours sand down your back—
that whole time this light is shining inside her.

Suddenly you know. This light
is Terry's goodness.
And no matter what she does or what anyone does to her,

this light is always there. Shining in Terry
even if she doesn't know it.

Terry steps closer to the road. A can hits your arm.
You back into the bushes .
Go the fuck home. Get the fuck away.
The light doesn't disappear.

For the first time you think that maybe Terry
can't help doing what she does. She's mean to you
because her mother is so mean to her. She spits at you
because someone spits at her, calls you curse words
because her mother hollers curse words at her.
Terry probably doesn't even want to be mean.
She just can't help it. The truth is
that inside Terry is goodness.

You know that now and will never forget.
And not only that. Somehow you know
this goodness is inside of everybody!
Every single person. Even Terry's mother.
Even Donna Fagliarini and Mrs. Cadave
and the principal who wishes your family was dead.
Even they have a flame of goodness in them.

Terry runs out of cans to throw. Turns her back and walks away.
You go back to where your horse is waiting.
Lift her from the prickers and ride her home giddyup fast.
Think about how happy your mother will be
to find out that Terry doesn't want to be mean.
That she isn't mean deep inside.
The truth is she has goodness inside her.
Everybody does.

II.

Your mother slaps you when you tell her.
She doesn't want to hear about the flame. That you saw it and it's real.
Real as the onions she was cutting into small pieces
that made your eyes sting as soon as you came into the kitchen.
You don't understand why instead of being happy she is furious.
Why she wants to *beat this narishkeit out of you*.
Just wait, she says. *Your father will teach you to talk like this*
about antisemites. Goodness shmoodness.

She tells him soon as he comes in from the coops.
He makes you sit down. They yell about how dangerous it is
to think like this, to *believe people are good*.
The next thing you'll tell me the Nazis are good.
She slaps you again. Says it's for your own good. They don't want you
to be *foolish enough to think people like Terry who hate Jews can be good*.
Your father says *good* like it's an impossible thing for Terry to be.
You are a naïve girl, he hollers, *who won't survive in this world*
with ideas like this.

You try to tell them they are wrong. But they just holler louder.
So you stop trying to convince them.
You just listen to them try to change you.
Maybe when they think you learned your lesson, they'll
let you leave the kitchen. But not yet.
Your father walks back and forth. Doesn't even notice
the ash from his cigarette falling to the floor.

Do you understand how dangerous it is to think such things?!
You nod the smallest nod. The only way they will let you escape
is if you act like you agree with them, like they are right, and
you are wrong. Like they know best.

But you know what you saw. *Are sure of it.*
It makes you feel happy to know about the goodness.
Even though it's also confusing. Because how could Hitler
have goodness inside him?
And why does Terry keep hating you?

You never try again to tell your parents about
the goodness in people.
They will *never* believe you. If they did, maybe
they wouldn't be so sad all the time.
Maybe they would even have a little hope.
But no matter what, you won't ever forget,
long as you live. The flame you saw in the middle of Terry.
The light of her goodness.

suddenly the window by your bed opens
to the unspeakable consolation of lilacs

you press your cheek to the screen
fall asleep with your head on the sill

wish not to miss a moment
of their brief fragrant lives

I see you on the roof of chicken coop number 4.
Your father told you to climb the ladder then
took the ladder away. From below he is yelling. *Jump!*
You want to cry but don't dare. If you cry it will all be harder.

Jump he insists. *Do you think I would let you get hurt?*
But you don't jump. You can't, relieved that he doesn't see
the butterflies more like bats in your belly
and the tears you try to keep from flooding your eyes.
What, you don't trust your father?
He says it like you not jumping is hurting him.
It's not that, you think to say, not making the words come out.
Still you don't jump.

You think of when he lifted you up out of the water at Iona Lake
and put you on the tall dock that sticks way out into the water.
He dove back under, disappearing long enough in the dark purple water
that you thought maybe he drowned
until all of a sudden, he popped up. Laughing.
Rubbing his red eyes that without glasses make him into a stranger—
like those times he wakes screaming from a nightmare
and your mother holds him close in the hushed house.
Jump! he called out from down in the lake. *I'll catch you.*
And finally, you did. You jumped into the deep dark lake
where instead of catching you, he backed up farther and farther.
Just swim to me. And you paddled like your life depended on it.

No child of mine is going to be afraid, he shouts now. Looking up,
looking angry. Like he is ashamed of you. And you know
that he is. Because you would not have been as brave as him
in The War. You probably would have been one of those fools

on the bank of the Volga River whose hands froze to their shovels
and had to be cut off or who were afraid to swallow
a piece of frozen dog thawed in a secret fire. You who are too scared
to just jump off the roof of coop number 4 with your very own father
standing there, promising that he will catch you,
that he would never do anything to hurt you.
He just wants to make sure you have
what it takes
to survive.

Under the willow with Lucky,
your hand on her warm breathing body.
Her head heavy on your leg. You sit
back-to-back with the willow always here.
How good, these best friends.
That they don't talk like people is even better. They listen.
Answer with their love.   Their touch on your skin.
Their eyes seeing you.
Like now when Lucky lifts her head and stares at you, eyes glistening.
Two brilliant brown marbles clear as light.
You stare back.

All of a sudden you know—maybe the biggest secret of any.
God is hiding *inside* Lucky.
In her dark hairy animal body. Deep in her belly.
One of God's best ever hiding places.
You know, too, that the way in is through Lucky's eyes.
Not going in with your body, but with *wanting to go in*. With believing.
The way in looks small but the space where God is
deep inside Lucky is not small. It opens wide. Big as the world.
Bigger.
You just know this. Wonder if you are the only one.

Lucky can't tell anyone this secret.
Neither will you. No one would believe you anyway.
But not only that. You don't *want* everyone to know.
Not even to know the hint you didn't realize was a hint.
DOG is GOD spelled backwards. Proof it's true!

Until now, you thought God was mostly up in the sky
on an invisible throne guarded by angels.

Or flying over places where people, especially children, need help.
But God is right here. Invisible. But *so close.* Inside
what looks like just an ordinary regular dog.
God just waiting for you to find out how close.
To know that anytime you want to talk to God, you can.
Under the weeping willow branches and sky.
No prayerbook in your hands. No synagogue roof between you.
No long time waiting for angel guards to
let you into the room with the throne to ask questions.
To say *Thank you. I'm sorry. Please help.*

You usually stay careful not to bother God.
Don't want to waste God's time.
But inside Lucky, God seems in no hurry. Listens patiently.
Just like your best friends.

When your hand lifts with Lucky's breaths, you wonder
if you are feeling God breathe.

On the dirt path between the coops,

heart skipping with joy even before your legs do,

you make your way to the open meadow out past all seven coops.

A wide field, circled with waiting trees whose laughter

you can almost hear swirling over the tips of sizzling,

golden grasses, so tall they reach your armpits.

All you have to do is squat to be gone, to be invisible

to anybody who might come. But no one ever does.

You can be alone there.

You call this part of the farm *The Ranch*. From the song

Home Home on the Ranch, where seldom is heard a discouraging word

and the skies are not cloudy all day.

That is not at all like it was in The War.

Then there were *only* cloudy skies. No flowers grew.

And all the words were discouraging.

You know just some of the words from the home on the ranch song.

Wonder if sometimes you mix in words from that other one

She'll be comin round the mountain when she comes.

You pretend the ranch is the home that *she,* who you imagine is you,

is comin' to find.

Today on the ranch, the sun is so hot you decide to take off your clothes.

First one old Ked, then the other, throwing each in different directions

far as you can. Then your socks one at a time that don't go as high or far

as your Keds. You wiggle your free toes.

Pull your blouse over your head. Toss it high out of sight.

The white *hemdella* under your blouse. Your shorts.

You watch the pieces of yourself disappear.

Only thing you keep on is your panties so the grass

won't feel pokey and bugs won't crawl into your peshy.

Down on your belly, you press your lips to kiss the warm ground.
Wish you belonged here the way the grass does.
Elbows down, chin on the shelf your palms make,
you watch ants crawl over and under arched grass bridges.
Try to be quiet as them on their long trips from home to home
with supplies it takes so many to carry.
You press your ear to the ground to hear the rumble of the earth's belly.
Roll over on your back. Look up at the upside-down blue bowl of sky
filled with emptiness and clouds.

You stand. Take off your panties so you can be
all the way naked.
Now comes the spinning.
You stand up tall, feet bottoms pressing down strong.
Arms wide like you are a gigantic letter T.

You lean your head back, face up.
You don't look straight at the sun but know
it's smiling a huge smile. You smile back.
Begin to turn.
Slow at first.
Then faster.
You spin and spin and spin
until the towering trees are spinning all around you.
The clouds spinning over you. The whole wide world
spinning around you.
No better place to be.

Dizzy after a long time spinning, you tip,
fall back. The warm ground catches you,
keeps on spinning, a spinning plate with you on it
lifted up to the light.

I see you on your way to the library, not nearly often enough
in the back seat of the red and black Chrysler,
barely able to keep all those excited butterflies—as many
as the books on the shelves—inside your nine-year-old belly.

Words are more important to you than food, your parents
say often about you and *your love affair with books.*
You don't know what a love affair is. But you do know
you love books and it's true you would rather read then eat.

Your mother drops you off alone as usual,
takes your brother and little sister with her to the
Kosher butcher, the shoemaker, Sears Roebuck.
Ivy vines cling to the old red brick library to which you'd
attach yourself too, live here, if you could.
You climb the steep steps, wish that by magic
one and a half hours would turn into one and a half days,
even weeks, which still would not be enough time to
touch all the books, one by one by one.

The door opens and there they are. Lined up in rows
on shelves that go from the floor almost to the ceiling.
Rooms full of books. You can't help the tears of happiness
that rush into your eyes, wipe them with your sleeve.
You need to see to make your way to the A's in
the Young Adult room where a few visits back
you decided you would read every single book in the library.
You knew it would take a very long time because you only
come to the library maybe once in a month.
And there are still so many A's left. But you won't give up.
How can you when you haven't even gotten to the B's?

Last time you were here, you found Louisa May Alcott.
The only woman in the Authors Card Game.
Now you take three of Louisa's books, hug them close,
tiptoe across the creaky floor in this quietest of places
where your mother would not be allowed to holler,
which is probably why she never comes in.
You put the treasure on the table, surprised like always
that you can have these for free, that all you have to do
is show the library card you signed with your name.
You are the only one in the family who has one, who
even wants a library card. You don't tell the librarian
when you pass the books across the desk-table toward her
that you will sleep with these books, that in your bed
after everyone is asleep, you will slowly move your hand
along the spine of one, put another under your pillow,
press the third to your chest.

The librarian rolls the numbers to the right date,
opens each back cover, pulls out the Date Due card,
stamps it, then slips the lined card back into its paper pocket.
You don't say that later, when your brother is snoring
and your sister is dreaming, you'll open one of these books,
close your eyes, press your nose into its pages,
breathe in deep the book's scent. Because books
are not just for reading, you don't tell her, though
being a librarian, she must know. They are for loving.

You walk into the kitchen to tell them.
Your mother at the sink. Your father at the table,
bent over his newspaper. You clear your throat.
Say, kind of loud, *I have something to tell you.*

Your mother turns, your father raises his head.
Both look at you. Curious not angry.
Not impatient either like
more important things are waiting for them.

Suddenly you imagine saying *Never mind.* Walking out.
But you stay. Look down at the checkered floor and
get ready to say what feels as real as
the three wooden steps that lead up to the screen door,
real as the screen door, as your hands.

One day, you begin,
I am going to write things that make people laugh and cry.
You don't wait to hear what they will say.
You are not asking their permission.

Your words and this knowing you could not keep inside
hang behind in the kitchen at the same time
as they go with you, inside you. Where you will keep them
safe.

Your family acts like it's a normal thing not to look up at it.
As if the sky was not the most changing
beautiful thing in the whole world.
Here it is right over your chicken farm that is so far from everything
even from the other *greena* chicken farms in Vineland.
The huge sky. Above your small house just like it hangs over
the rich Kellogg horse farm with the tall white fence no one can see over
on the corner of Iona Road and the road Terry lives on.

The blue sky is over Terry's house and farm too.
Even when her mother yells mean words from the falling-down porch.
You don't know what kind of farm Terry lives on.
You never see any animals in the part wire, part wood pens,
the shape of tall triangles. Just two really skinny black cats.

Today, riding by Terry's house on your bike-horse,
you see a big girl, maybe Terry's sister, stumble out of
one of the small cage coops. Her belly huge as a barrel.
Barefoot in the mud, she tips one way then another
Fuckin mud shithole! you hear her shout. You think
maybe she's drunk, the way the mad words come out and
how she can't walk straight.

You hear a different voice holler *You deserve what you got, whore.*
A no-good little bastard like you.
It's Terry's mother leaning on the broken railing.

The sad girl bends over and throws up.
Throws up more. Put her hands under her heavy belly.
Drops to her knees.
The blue sky over her too.

You don't like what your mother is saying to your father
on the way to your Uncle Maier and Tanta Rootie's house in Vineland.
Maybe your mother thinks you can't hear her
by the open window in the back seat of the red and black Chrysler.
But you can.

It's not the first time they say mean things about Rootie.
How she always wears a house dress. The same *shmata*
even when she goes out, which Rootie hardly ever does,
and Uncle Maier gave up trying to make her do.
They talk about how Rootie drags her feet in her worn-out
shtekshikh. Head down. Never looking anyone in the eyes.
They feel sorry that Maier has Rootie for his wife.
Like a child she is, they are saying again.
What kind of mother can she be to the boys?

You're glad the visits are only once in a blue moon
because of how they treat Rootie.
Even though it's a sin against *Thou Shalt Honor Thy Mother,*
you hate that your mother acts better than Rootie.
Because your mother's taller. Because she polishes her nails.
Puts on lipstick. Wears a girdle and high heels.
Always dresses up for the *greena* parties that Rootie
doesn't even want to go to. Rootie is happiest in her kitchen.
Making *lokshen, rugalach,* or *kugel.*
That's where you like best being with Rootie, too.

Whenever you visit you stay in her kitchen,
just big enough for the two of you.
Mein Annalah, she says, clapping her hands together, eyes wide
like someone just turned on the light in her dark little kitchen.

She wipes her hands on her apron. Cups them around your cheeks.
Bist azoy shein, such a beautiful girl, she says,

looking into your eyes, kissing your forehead.
You don't see Rootie very often. But every time you do,

it's always like that. Like the two of you share a secret love.
You wash and dry dishes side by side. Arms touching.

Watch Rootie measure this and that into what she's cooking
that always tastes good. Better than what your mother,

who mostly just boils things, cooks.
When you are together Rootie usually starts to sing in Yiddish. Softly.

Looking up to wink at you. Singing is Rootie's other favorite thing
besides cooking and listening to her oldest son sing.

Rootie told you once that she loves *Opera.*
Do you know what opera is, sheina Annalah?

You shook your head. She just smiled, kissed your cheek,
then started singing again.

When Rootie sings she's in another world. A happier one, you think,
than her regular one with your parents in it criticizing her.

Now from the kitchen, next to Rootie, you hear your mother
laugh loud at something Uncle Maier says. Hear your father

complain about Shattuck the feed man, about how much it costs
for a bag of feed and what's happening to the farmers who can't pay.

Uncle Maier can't pay, you heard your father tell your mother one night.
That's why his coops are empty, and he has to move to Brooklyn.

To make a living a different way. *Rootie is no help,* they always blame,
your mother so proud that she can *understand business like a man.*

But Rootie, she says, *what does she understand?*

How your mother talks about Rootie goes against
what she tries to teach you about *Derech Eretz, Respect.*

Respect is the most important thing there is, your parents say.
Derech Eretz makes a mensch a mensch.

But when it comes to Rootie, your mother doesn't have any respect.

Rootie, like she's waking you up from a dream, touches your cheek now.
Winks. Takes the potholders you made her,
lifts the hot Pyrex dish of kugel and walks from the small kitchen
to the table, looking down, dragging her feet. Like she's
pretending to be who they think she is.
Rootie doesn't smile when she puts the plate on the table.
Be careful, it's hot, she says without looking up.
Then she goes back to the kitchen. She never sits with them
to eat what she cooked, no matter how many times
Uncle Maier says *Please Rootie, please come sit down.*

On the way home, you make believe you're asleep
like your brother and little sister really are. You hear
your mother say *What a rachmunus for Maier.* Such a pity
he has to put up with Rootie.
Did you see how she couldn't even look me in the eye?
You know that Rootie *can* look in people's eyes.
She looks in yours all the time. Maybe Rootie
doesn't want to look in your mother's eyes.
You want to say it's not true Rootie is a *shanda*,
someone to be ashamed of. You don't blame Rootie
for hiding in her little kitchen, for not even
turning on its lights when your parents come to her house.

You don't try to change their minds. One reason is
they will just say you are *naïve*. What they always say about you.
That you don't understand how the world *really* is.
The other bigger reason you don't try to change them
is that you believe Rootie wants
to keep secret who she really is.

I.

It is morning.

Daylight wakes you suddenly again.

You wonder how it does that without ever touching you.

You open one eye, close it. Don't move.

So no one, especially your mother, will know you are awake.

You lie still as dead to have just a little more time here.

Any minute she will come to the bedroom door.

Break the small quietness you are hiding inside of.

She won't see it, but like always she will break it.

She will turn on the light in the center of the ceiling

like it's the sun and she is making it rise to start the day.

You know what happens to lazy people?

They don't amount to anything.

You won't want to move. But you will be afraid

to make her angrier if you don't.

She isn't at the door yet. It's still quiet.

A tiny bit of time left to be alone,

under your blankets and in your own mind.

No one bossing you. Saying you're selfish

to like being alone.

Just you in this quiet place where

you aren't doing anything wrong yet.

II.

Esther, your mother, pauses in the doorway to your room.

Like an angel she cannot see but can feel, I—

a woman now—blow gently on the nape of her neck.

A warm soothing breath, so soothing,
she lowers her arm from the light switch.
From under your blanket, you hear her go.
Listen for the silence. Start to breathe more easily

Esther walks to the screen door. Opens it slowly.
Steps out into the morning air. She sighs. Looks up.
And for now, instead of feeling only loss,
the absence of the ones she is always grieving,
she feels a presence. The presence that kept her going
when all odds were against her. When disguised as a devout Catholic,
she prayed the rosary morning to night,
sliding one bead then another between her fingers,
lips moving soundlessly. That same presence with her
when she was hidden beneath the floorboards of a barn.

It is not only sorrow that stands with her this morning,
when instead of yelling at her oldest daughter she lets the child,
a girl she is grateful did not live through a War, sleep in.

Esther wonders if it might be alright—not dangerous, even safe—
to let her children sleep, wake, and play without remembering.
Without doing everything right to keep bad things
from happening. Or to somehow change what did.
They are innocent, she says out loud.
Looking up like she was giving her face to God.
Without shame for having survived.
Without knowing why it all happened as it did.

Letting herself be loved.

COLORS

What a thrill for you to flip open
the top of the biggest box of Crayola Crayons there is.
48 COLORS! Bought at the Elmer 5 &10 after a long time.
With money saved up from packing eggs in the cellar.
A Whole Castle of Crayons.
Each one in its place with perfect points and names you never heard.
BURNT SIENNA. GOLD OCHRE. LAVENDER.
A green family: OLIVE GREEN. BLUE GREEN. YELLOW GREEN.
Just plain GREEN. The one you know best. Color of summer grass
with dewdrops on its tips that have no color because clear
is not a color. Though sometimes there are rainbows inside clear.
You know grass can also be brown green or green brown when
it hasn't rained for a long time or in winter, underneath snow.
You can't find Green-Brown or Brown-Green in the box
even after checking one by one by one.

RAW UMBER makes you laugh, saying it makes you think of burps.

You knew even before you opened the box about many blues.
You know from looking at the sky. Blue so light it's almost white.
But there's no Blue-White or White-Blue crayon.
You've heard people say baby blue and sky blue, which you think
must be the same—how the sky looks when it's the most peaceful,
just a few white puffs of clouds floating in a blue that
makes you feel you don't have to be afraid. You can
lie down on your back in the grass, close your eyes and
nothing bad will happen. That blue isn't in the box either.

You see a dark blue tip. Hope it will match the sky at night. Try it out.
Not dark enough. Blue-Black is the crayon you need.
You search again just in case it's there. Find BLACK. Close but

not quite right because the night sky isn't really black
though it looks like it sometimes, like a huge black cloth
with tiny holes the stars burn through so we will see them.
So we won't be afraid and think there is no light those nights
when the moon hides herself. You wonder if
maybe it's impossible to color the moods of the sky
with any crayon. But you aren't sure. So you search out
all the ones with bluish tips, being really careful because these crayons
are skinny and easy to break if you're not careful
like your brother and sister aren't. In their hands, crayons snap.
Their paper coats tear. They don't get put back in their right rows.
These 48 are going to be just for you.
You'll sleep with this box to protect them.

You turn each blue-tipped crayon sideways to see its name.
PRUSSIAN BLUE. CERULEAN BLUE. AZURE BLUE.
COBALT BLUE. MEDIUM BLUE. TURQUOISE BLUE seems
the wildest, the most free of the blues. Its silly name.
How it looks on paper when you make letters or draw a picture with it.
TURQUOISE, you are pretty sure, probably has more fun
than most of the other crayons in the box.

Blues all put back, you go across each row, pulling out
every single crayon. One at a time. Say its name.
Even the colors you already know like ORANGE. RED. YELLOW. WHITE.

With colors you are meeting for the first time today,
you write your favorite letters in the alphabet
on a velvety white paper napkin. Watch the colors sink in.

There is one crayon you don't want to put back.
Its name like a Queen's. MAGENTA.
You make a rainbow shape with it like a bridge.
Want to walk on that bridge. To rest there.

No other crayon in the gigantic box
makes you feel like MAGENTA does.
Like this color matches you. But not what people can see.
MAGENTA is what people can't see about you.

You don't worry about your mother when she is
getting ready for one of the *greena* parties.

She says the *greena*, refugees and orphans like her,
understand like other people can't.
You don't have to explain. Everybody knows without
needing to talk about it.
If you start to cry, no one is surprised.
They know how it feels to be alone in the park,
like I was on East New York Avenue with two babies,
no grandparents or anybody else to be happy with me.
Nobody to be proud with me when my child did something new.
Oh, your father, of course. But he was away morning to night.

You know that's why they left New York and bought the farm.
Your father thought she would be less lonely.
He would be closer. They would have other *greena* nearby—
a whole settlement of *greena* who also bought chicken farms
after World War II. These new refugees on top of the Jews
who came to Vineland between the wars. To escape pogroms in Russia.
To settle the land. To make a new life.

The Russian Jews came with big ideas, your father says
like he's making fun of them almost every time
you drive down Landis Avenue. *They wanted socialism. But now*
it's Epstein the Dentist. Shapiro the Doctor. Their socialism
went out the window. You think he wishes he could be like them.
Someone with enough education not to be a farmer.
At least someone who had enough money to buy a farm in Vineland
like the other *greena*, instead of your farm so many miles away
where no Jews live and everyone thinks Jews have horns they're hiding.

The *greena* who go to the parties are all part of the JPFA,
which stands for Jewish Poultry Farmers Association.
You wonder how they picked such an American-sounding name.

Your mother takes all afternoon to get ready.

Polishing her nails comes first. She sits on the toilet with the top down.
Smears the red polish off her pointy fingernails
with Cutex polish remover and white cotton.
The whole bathroom stinks, even the hallway.
But your mother can't tell without a sense of smell.
You stand just inside the door and watch,
holding your nose. She doesn't mind.
It's like she's in a different world.
One without any Nazis in it.
She's wearing a blue see-through nightgown, her breasts
like two huge grapefruits, nipples pale pink not dark like yours.
Because she had red hair once.
Polish kids called her *carrot head*. She hated it.
Her mother said her hair was beautiful,
but she didn't believe it.
In the end red hair, a cross, and a new name
helped her save herself.
She waves her hands around. Blows on her red nails.
When they're all the way dry, she paints her toes.
No trip to the beauty parlor today to get her hair set.
She combs it herself. Hairspray tickles the inside of your nose.
The face she makes in the medicine cabinet mirror shows
she doesn't like how her hair looks. She mumbles
something you can't understand. Probably in Polish.

Next is her girdle. Your father helps hook it while she holds her breath.
Slowly she pulls up one nylon stocking then the other. Extra careful

not to make *a run,* a line that shoots up and *looks cheap,* she says
while concentrating hard on attaching her nylon stocking to a hook
hanging from her girdle.
Back in front of the medicine cabinet mirror, it's time
for the makeup she always says she has no idea
how to put on right. Light blue on top of eyelids. Pink powder
on cheeks. Orange lipstick that always gets on her teeth.
You never tell her when you see it there in case she might feel
embarrassed. Or mad that she did it wrong.
Your father fastens a gold chain around her neck.
He bought it from a man he knew in Poland before The War,
a jeweler now in New York City. Her one gold necklace.
They hide it between parties to keep it safe.

His getting dressed takes only a few minutes.
Pressed pants. A clean *hemdella* underneath
his ironed white shirt. Cufflinks he lets you help him put on.
The tie you don't ever ask to help knot.
Shiny black shoes he polished earlier, pulled over his white socks.
Finally comes the black suit jacket that besides to *greena* parties
he only wears to synagogue.

You like how handsome he looks. How he winks at you and
whistles when your mother walks into the kitchen
wearing her high heel shoes. Looking so different than regular.
More fancy. A little embarrassed. But also, she is smiling
at how your father is looking at her. Like he is hungry
and she is something yummy
he wants to eat.

Tonight the *greena* come all the way
to your house in Elmer for their Saturday night party
even though they always get lost on the way.

From your bedroom, you sneak peeks
through the crack between your door and the wall.
Everyone all dressed up drinking schnapps.
Tall Bluma whose red hair reminds you of flames
is wearing a strapless green evening gown
that makes you think of a mermaid, and looks like it might
fall down any minute so her *chitchis* will show.

Your father is acting different. More carefree.
How he dances with Bluma—arms moving like he's in water.
Bluma, a queen in her shimmery green gown
pouring down over her shape all the way
to the green glittery high heels she kicks off,
laughing.
Her toenails painted the color of blood.

You put your hand flat across the top of your nose
so all you can see are Bluma's naked shoulders.
You pretend Bluma is *all the way* naked, except for two small round
pearls stuck to her ears.
Bluma's shoulders are covered with freckles.
You watch her hot pink lips when she laughs. A lot more laughing
than your mother who almost never laughs and for sure not loud and free
like Bluma. Their only thing alike is that your mother has freckles too.
She used to have red hair too
but it turned brown in The War. And stayed brown.
Like her sense of smell, your mother's red hair never came back.

After the party is over and everyone goes home, your mother
who thinks you are asleep whispers to your father with an angry hiss
that she doesn't like when he gets drunk.
You *do* like it if it means seeing him dance like he did.
Are you still surprised, she asks him,
to know how Bluma survived the war?
Her voice is that way it gets
when you can almost taste the bitter in it.

You wish you knew what she meant.
How beautiful happy Bluma stayed alive
when most people didn't? You're so glad she did.
You wonder if it's because Bluma kept laughing.
Even though you know that wouldn't really keep Nazis away.
You just wish it could.

I see you stretched on your belly in the field
by the tangled blueberries. You're waiting
for the Nazis to attack. For their tall black boots
to trample the tender grass that doesn't hurt anything,
that only loves your feet, the sun, the rain.

You don't know from which direction they will come
when they finally find you
after their march past the Statue of Liberty who
promised to protect your family.
But you're not sure you can really trust her.

You have nothing to fight with. Can just
watch for them. You wonder if there'll be time
to warn your mother and father. Maybe
you can throw yourself at the soldiers' feet
like meat to hungry animals and hope they will
be satisfied. If only long enough for your parents to
what? Where would they go?

You pull up your blouse, feel the grass tickle your belly.
Roll over. Look up at the sky.
At the clouds floating there, no matter the Stormtroopers.
You start to float on the clouds. Imagine a world
without Stormtroopers. Where The War is *really over.*
Where you a girl can dare to close your eyes, to feel
breezes rushing across the field, soft and gentle
on your bare belly. No reason to be afraid.

You let the heaviness of your body sink more into the ground.
Let the fear of Nazis coming lift off a little bit.

What if you can trust
the peace of the sky,
the kind breezes, the dream
that this might be
a free country.

You call them Aunt Lilly and Uncle Morris, but they aren't really related.
Not like Tanta Rae, Tanta Rootie, or Uncle Avrom's wife Sarah who
you only saw once in a picture when he visited from Israel—
tucking you in every night with a kiss on your heads
he said was a stamp to send you across the world to Tanta Sarah.

Aunt Lilly is the only grown-up who talks to you about reading books.
Aunt Lilly and Uncle Morris drive to the farm from New York.
Maybe one time every year or every two. You wish it were every week.
Uncle Morris pays attention to children how most grown-ups don't.
As if he likes to be with children as much as with grown-ups.
He brings toys. Small things that are just right.

This time, a bag of rubber cowboys and Indians. Rubber horses too
(that you wish did not tip over when you put riders on them).
Uncle Morris gets down on the gray carpet in the living room
where you, Marty, and Shelly are allowed to play today because
company is over and it's easier for Uncle Morris to play on a floor
with a carpet. You pick the Indians. Marty the cowboys.
Count *1 2 3* then start the battle. Uncle Morris makes noises
to go with the game. Pretends he got shot with an arrow.
Falls over backwards dead. Opens one eye and whispers
It's okay to jump on me to bring me back to life.

After your parents say *Give Uncle Morris a break,*
another too-good-to-be-true part comes. Aunt Lilly
pats on a spot next to her for you to come sit there.
She's on the pink sofa just for company. A *sectional*, it's called.
Wrapped tight in clear plastic to keep it clean,
plastic that in the summer sticks to skin when you have shorts on,

like now. But to sit next to Aunt Lilly it's worth it
even if it will hurt later to peel yourself off.

Aunt Lilly and you will finally talk about books.
Just the two of you.
You move so close, your leg touches Aunt Lilly's. You tell her
how much you love *Black Beauty*. That the teacher reads it at lunchtime
almost every day. Sometimes you put your head down on your desk
to hide your crying when sad things happen in the story.
Listening to *Black Beauty* is the best thing about third grade,
you tell Lilly who nods a lot because she understands.
You don't tell her the other big reason you like when
Mrs. Cadave reads out loud. When she's reading, she forgets
to make fun of you. And when the kids are listening, they forget, too.

Besides both loving books, there's something else wonderful
about being close to Aunt Lilly on her once-in-a-blue-moon visits.
It's how she smells. Like those tiny white flowers, the littlest of bells
so good at hiding. Lilly says it's *perfume* you smell, made from
those little white flowers, perfume Uncle Morris buys for her.
When Uncle Morris hears you talking about how good Aunt Lilly smells,
he starts sniffing her like he was an animal and Lilly was too,
making her laugh and say *Oh Morris!*
Uncle Morris keeps sniffing. *Ah, now I can smell it!* he calls out.
Lily-in-the-Bronx perfume. From Macy's.
He picks up Lilly's purse with his teeth and away he goes
on his hands and knees like a dog with a bone.
Aunt Lilly doesn't get mad, just says *Oh my. We can't take him
anywhere, can we?* Then she kisses the top of your head.

You don't mind feeling Lilly breathe on you when you are very close.
Different from your mother who has so much trouble with breathing.
Her nose always getting plugged and needing blowing.

The mucus in her throat. The sounds she makes like breathing is hard
work. Worst of all is her bad breath. You move away not to smell it.
Never saying that's why you move away.
The time you had a big hot fever and she brought you to sleep in her bed,
you didn't sleep a wink. She snored all night, making swampy sounds.
In the morning when she leaned over to kiss your forehead, her way to
check your temperature, you tried not to wrinkle your nose,
not to show how much you don't like being that close to her body.

In between Uncle Morris and Aunt Lilly visiting
which is a big in-between, you sit under your favorite pine tree
with its wide, needly skirt, one of the best places to read
because it's harder for people to find you there, to make you stop.
More secret than by the willow where they always think to look.
You hold your book up to your chest. Close your eyes.
Feel how Lilly smells. How she looks at you. How she smiles
when you tell her what you like about a book.
How she listens
then tells you what she likes.

SAFE

I.

You won't go back to Jacksonville School
ever again, your father tells you one morning.
You get scared it's because he killed the principal.
But he doesn't say he did. And he would probably tell if he had, so
maybe you can just feel happy.
You'll be going to Camden Hebrew Day School, he says.
A school where they want Jews.

II.

Camden is almost an hour ride from the farm each way.
Not on a yellow school bus. The bus to Camden
has huge, dark windows and cozy tall seats.
Some kids even fall asleep on the ride. Of course, you don't.
It's hard to get used to no one pulling your hair.
Holding your arms down. Searching for horns.
Nobody says you stink. Takes your lunchbox. Holds their noses.
Not a single person makes fun of you
for being different. You keep waiting for it to happen.
But it doesn't.
It takes a lot of rides going back and forth
to start believing that it's not going to happen on this bus,
to stop looking around for who might be sneaking up behind you.
Nobody ever does.

One day you lean back in your tall seat and close your eyes.
The first bunch of times you do it, you wait only a few seconds
before opening your eyes again. Then one night
when it's the dark on the way home and extra cozy,
you close your eyes and don't open them right away.
You let the bus just take you for a ride. Feel it carry you along

like nothing bad will happen. That's the day you decide
that maybe you don't have to be afraid on this bus.

To make the long ride go faster, everybody sings.
Songs you never heard before. *99 Bottles of Beer on the Wall.*
You Can't Get to Heaven in Moshe's Car or *Miriam's* or
someone else's car whose name the kids put into the song.
You don't think their cars really stop at bars, then figure out
it's not a teasing song and start to sing along.
Nobody makes fun of how you sing or if
you get the words or numbers mixed up.
Nobody waits for you to make mistakes.
The other kids don't even especially notice you. Not in a bad way.

You're just another girl on the bus who nobody makes fun of.
And Marty is just another boy. Nobody snatches his *yamaka* off his head
and throws it out the window like on the yellow bus to Jacksonville.
On the long road to Camden, a person can be someone with nothing
to be ashamed of. Sometimes you're ashamed anyway because
you're used to it, to being ashamed. It's hard to get used to
no one saying you should be.
You wonder while you sing along with the other kids
if you ever will feel as free as they are, laughing, falling asleep,
seeming *not to know* what it's like to be so different
that you almost always would rather be invisible.

III.

Around Chanukah time, the fourth grade teacher tells your mother
you are *Advanced.* You seem bored in fourth grade and should
skip into fifth after the holiday. Your parents say okay.

You are still in fourth grade when boiling water spills
all over Rachel's leg who is in fourth grade too and

who is the fourth grade teacher's daughter.

You feel sorry for Rachel but even more sorry for her mother

who turns almost as red as Rachel's leg, shakes, cries, and

keeps repeating, *Thank God, no one else got hurt!*

It's the first *Terrible Accident* you are in the same room with

when it happens. When someone gets hurt so bad

they have to be taken away to the hospital in an ambulance.

Rachel doesn't die. She doesn't even seem so changed

when she returns to fourth grade. Except for the burn marks on her leg.

But her mother, the teacher, is sadder than she ever used to be.

A few weeks later you skip into fifth grade.

IV.

In fifth grade there is a shy boy named Aaron with dark hair and

blue eyes, you think, but aren't sure. He sits in the last row

and is really good at arithmetic like you.

You wish Aaron would talk to you. But he never does.

Sometimes you wonder if he is looking at your ponytail

and thinking he likes you. But when you sneak a look at him,

he's just bent over his desk. Probably doing arithmetic problems.

V.

Your brother in second grade starts to get into trouble at recess.

The teacher writes your parents a letter that you help them read.

Because of Martin's bad behavior, I may have to give your son

a U in Conduct. Your parents don't know what a U in Conduct means

and neither do you, except you know it's a bad thing.

Martin is much bigger than the other second graders.

He must learn to control himself. He is hurting other children.

Your mother starts crying even before you finish the letter.

He also has trouble pronouncing his R's correctly.

Your mother's head hangs down so low, it looks like
it might drop into her lap. She believes all Marty's problems are
her fault. Your father acts like it's a good thing not a bad one
that Marty is beating up other kids on the playground.

At night in your bed, you think about what the teacher wrote.
It's true Marty is big. He wears Husky size and he's almost as tall
as you are even though he's two and a half years younger.
But the truth is Marty isn't mean. He isn't hurting the other kids
on purpose. He just doesn't know how big he is
and that he's strong enough to hurt anyone. You know this
because he gets surprised that he can hurt you now more than
you can hurt him, which you have been trying to keep a secret.
So you can keep bossing him around.

VI.
You learn a lot of things in fifth grade. Torah. Praying.
Especially the *Shmoneh Esreh* which means eighteen
and stands for eighteen blessings, some of them so special
you have to bend your knees and bow your head
when you whisper them to God.
You learn harder arithmetic too. Geography.
Penmanship is the best thing of all. Connecting the letters to each other
feels like learning magic tricks.

In fifth grade in Camden Day School, you stop worrying
that the teacher will make you stand up and apologize
for disturbing the class. You are part of the class.
You might be invisible to Aaron but you are not
invisible to the teacher and you don't
even want to be.

In your bedroom darkened so the measles won't make you blind,
light sneaks in from behind the venetian blinds and under
the bedroom door. Your eyes by now, used to the dark.

You see the Queen Esther dress hanging on the inside of the door.
Pink with layers of ruffles trimmed with sparkly sequins. So long
it touched the floor when you put it on before the measles came
and took away the chance forever to go to
the one-time-in-a-year Purim party and maybe win for Best Costume.

It took a few months for your parents to sew Queen Esther's dress
on their Singer Sewing Machine. Mostly they only make
necessary things. Blouses. Skirts. Once a pink wool winter coat
with shiny pink buttons like Necco wafers.
The whole time they were sewing Queen Esther's dress
your father kept saying *Don't get your hopes up.* That's because
he is president now of the Jewish Poultry Farmers Association
and they are making the party. *So, my child, no matter how good
your costume, you won't be able to win.*
But you didn't give up. Until tonight.

Your parents went to the party without the three of you,
leaving you home in the dark. Jasper who works on the farm
is in the bungalow in case of an emergency.

Your brother is snoring. Your sister asleep.
The beautiful, sparkling Queen Esther dress, quiet.
But you know the JPFA Purim party isn't quiet.
When Haman's name comes during the reading of the *Megillah*,
the Purim story, everyone—the kids and the grown-ups—

will shake noisemakers extra hard. Haman was the Hitler of that time.
Their names both starting with H like in Hate.
What they both stood for, especially hate for the Jewish people.
Haman wanted to hang every single Jew. Or to poison them.
To rid the kingdom of Jewish vermin
like Hitler trying to clean out Germany and the whole world.
No more filthy Jews.

Queen Esther, who your mother is named after,
was the hero in Haman's time. She convinced King Ahasuerus
to spare her people. It was a close call.
Esther could have been hung.
Her faith and her Uncle Mordechai gave her courage.
Mordechai is your brother Marty's Hebrew name
that he got from your father's father.
Probably Esther did not have a pink dress anything like yours.
But when you put the dress on after it was *finally* all finished,
you felt courage like Queen Esther's.
Now you're trying hard not to feel sad.
And you're not doing a good job.
Purim is just this one night. Your only chance to wear the dress.
To feel brave and beautiful like Queen Esther. Instead,
you're wearing pajamas. Trying not to scratch itchy measles.

At this very minute, the children at the party must be
shaking their noisemakers. Soon they will eat the candy
that rains down from a paper donkey
they took turns hitting with the handle of a broom.

You stare at the light sliding in under the bedroom door.
Wonder if the measles really can
make you blind.

It snows so much the lights go off in the house.
You have to shine flashlights at night. *No electricity* is what it's called,
your mother tells you. Soon *the house will be as cold*
as the inside of a refrigerator.
You start wearing snow pants all the time, even sleep in them.
Your mother can't cook anymore. You don't mind eating just cereal
until the milk runs out. One day, your father tells your mother
you all have to move into the bungalow where
the once-in-a-while farm helpers live.
Better than a house with no water and light,
to be in the small bungalow, he says, *with a coal stove to help*
keep warm, to melt snow to drink.

Your mother doesn't want to go. But agrees when it gets colder.
She packs the cereal, the cans in the closet, a can opener. Empties out
what's left in the refrigerator which is hardly anything because your
father started putting things like the cream cheese out in the snow.
She packs forks and spoons, wraps cups and plates in towels.
Pretty soon the march starts to the bungalow.

Your father goes first making footprints so deep they reach
the top of your legs. He sings at the front of the march, sounds happier
than he almost ever is. He says this reminds him of surviving in Siberia.
Only this is *much much easier.* No Russians with guns or whips.
Just keep marching, he says. And you do, behind your mother who is
right behind him, not happy like he is. You don't show that now you
are getting kind of happy too. Moving into the bungalow
is starting to feel like an adventure.
Your father found out on the transistor radio that there are no cars

on any of the roads. Wires down everywhere. It's too dangerous to
drive. Iona Road has snow so high no car could pass anyhow.
No school bus will be coming. *We'll be here for a while,* your father says
like he doesn't mind one single bit.
Just when he's about to pull open the falling-down door,
Gus opens it from the inside with a big smile on his face.
Gus helps on the farm and lives in the bungalow now.
Your father already told him about you all coming to live with him.
Gus is so happy he claps his hands a bunch of times and
does one of his silly dances on his toes, spinning around like
a ballerina in a music box. As usual, your father tells Gus to
stop acting like a child. For a few seconds Gus does stop.
Lowers himself off his toes. Then slowly he pulls his hand down
flat in front of his face like it was a shade being pulled down.
When his hand is all the way down past his neck, Gus has a serious look.
Right away he brings it up again like the curtain at Radio City Music
Hall. When it's all the way up he's smiling. Starts bouncing up and down
again. Your father rolls his eyes. Tries to ignore Gus.

Your mother unpacks the Heinz Baked Beans, the Campbell's
Cream of Mushroom Soup, Jolly Green Giant Peas and Jolly Green Giant
Corn, and the King Oscar sardines. A jar of Skippy Peanut Butter and
one of strawberry jelly. She never used to buy food in cans except for
tuna fish and sardines in a flat can whose top you have to roll back
just the right way not to spill the oil or cut your fingers.
She only started buying things in cans after some *greena* friends told her
Just try out the American easy way of eating. Everything from cans.
All Gus has in his bungalow kitchen is something called SPAM
and loaves of Wonder Bread—all he ever wants your mother to buy him
when she goes shopping no matter how much she tries to convince him
to eat other things. When she buys him bananas or apples or tuna fish, he
just leaves them on the back step of your house like they are gifts.
Sometimes he keeps the Wheaties.

Gus said his name was Santa Claus for a long time after he came
to live in the bungalow. You don't know how your father found out
his name is really Augustus Romano. After that your father said
he wouldn't call him Santa anymore. Gus looked so sad. Stopped talking.
One day, eyes full of tears, he whispered *Just call me Gus.* From then on
you all did.

The bungalow has three really small rooms in it.
Gus's cot is in the middle near the black coal stove.
Your mother and father will sleep on the floor in the back room
Marty, Shelly, and you in the front, blankets piled on the boards
held up by cinderblocks, more blankets over you.
You all wear extra clothes. Two pairs of socks. Two hats. Two sweaters.
Your winter jackets. Snow pants over regular pants over tights. Boots
kept on in the freezing room where you can see your breath.
You hope you won't need to pee until morning.
There's a small closet with a toilet in it, a chain you pull to flush.
But it doesn't work.

In the morning your father tells the three of you to come outside
so he can show you *where the bathroom is.* He points a little way from the
door. Says that's where to go. There's just snow there.
Caca, you cover it up with snow when you're finished. If you just pish,
never mind. You wish you could pee standing up like Marty.
Mad that girls can't. They all go back inside but you.
You pull down your snow pants then the pants under them then the tights
under the pants. You squat. Your pee makes a hole, turns the snow
yellowish. You squeeze dry the way your mother taught you in the woods
at A Lion's Beach and under the boardwalk. You are almost done when
your father comes hurrying from the bungalow holding a black pot,
a towel around its handle. He puts it in the snow to cool off. It hisses.
Melted snow, he says like he just won a prize. *All we need to survive!*
As long as you have water to drink, you can live. He kneels down.
Scoops water out of the pot with his cupped hands, splashes it on his face.

Oy Yoy Yoy! he screams laughing. *This is how I washed in Siberia.*
He says you should go next. You don't want to but have no choice.
You copy what he did, your bare hands freezing.

You start to like surviving the ways your father did in The War
as much as he likes teaching you how to survive. He seems
almost proud of you for being brave and doing what he shows you.
For your mother, you think maybe it was enough to survive once
and that's why she isn't excited about surviving again. She just wants
the electricity to come back. Though sometimes she comes
out of the bungalow and laughs at your father with his shirt off
washing his chest and arms with snow, screaming the whole time and
jumping up and down like he's on fire, only with cold.

The best part of all comes when your father teaches you
how to build a snow house and even helps you instead of hurrying
to do something more important. Your father, Marty, and you dig near
where the blueberries grow when it's not winter.
You make a big round deep space in the snow. Like a huge bowl.
Start rolling and piling up *Snow Rocks,* your father calls them.
One on top of the other. It takes a long time and so so many snow rocks
to make the sides high enough to block the cold wind. You leave
two holes in the wall of snow close to the ground. To crawl through.
Only kids can fit through those windows, not grown-ups.
You and Marty down on your bellies slide through like two fat snakes
wiggling their way in. Then you help pull Shelly through. You have to.
Your father said he wouldn't make the snow house *unless you promise to
include your sister.* Gus says you made an *igloo.* A funny new word
you think he made up.

The igloo doesn't melt. Even on the days of brightest sun. It's warmer
inside than outside. You never want to leave. You even convince
your mother to let you eat lunch in there. The way it works is if
Marty climbs in first. You pass the peanut butter and jelly sandwiches

in wax paper bags through the windows. Then climb in.
You both pull Shelly in like you promised.
Food tastes better in the snow house.
Strawberry jelly dripped on snow looks like blood for only a minute.
Then like yummy pink crystals. You eat *lots of snow.*

One sunny day, your mother comes to the igloo. Through the window
you watch her squeeze juice from the last orange left in the bungalow
over a bowl of snow. She scoops out three small cups of the orange treat.
Passes them one at a time through the igloo window. They sparkle.
It feels like you can taste the sunshine, taste your mother's smile.

You never worry about Gus hurting you. You know
he never will. That he would sooner hurt himself.
Like that time your father gave Gus extra money for his Christmas
and Gus used it to buy you all Monopoly,
the most expensive game at the Elmer 5 & 10
and too hard, Gus says, for him to play.
When you found a five-dollar bill crumpled up in the toe of your Ked,
you knew right away Gus was the one who put it there.

Gus says he doesn't need money.
Living in the bungalow close to all of you, he has
everything he needs, he always tells you.
He dances on his toes when your father
says it's time for a haircut at the Elmer Barber Shop.
Claps his hands when your mother brings him food.
Things your family doesn't eat because they aren't Kosher.
SPAM. Campbell's Beans & Franks. Oscar Mayer things.
Wonder Bread.

Gus says he never wants to go anywhere else. That he just
wants to be on the farm with all of you. Says he's *A happy man.*
Like Santa Claus. You wish you could still call him that.
It makes him so happy when you do.

What you don't like is how when your parents go to Philadelphia
to look for a new business and they stay overnight,
Gus, who is supposed to kind of take care of you,
pulls his pants down in the living room. Late. Always
after your brother and sister are asleep. Even his underpants.
And quick pushes his shmecky between his legs then
walks around the living room funny like he doesn't have a shmecky.

He asks you to watch. Asks a bunch of time if you like watching.
You don't.
You watch for just a few minutes so Gus won't look so sad if you don't.
When he asks again if you like it, you nod.
A really small nod. A lie nod. *You don't like it at all.*
You know it's wrong somehow. That he does it. That you watch.
Even if Gus never comes close to you. Doesn't touch you
or ever ask you to touch him. Only says *Watch me.*
It's part of how Gus is different from other people.
A grown-up who's like a kid, but not really.
Just not like a normal grown-up.

You never tell anyone. If you did, it would get Gus into trouble.
So you add what Gus does late to your pile of secrets.
If you kept all your secrets in a pocket instead of in your mind,
they would make the pocket stick out so much,
your parents would ask what was in it and find all your secrets.
But you know they can't find them in your mind,
which is another secret you've been keeping for a very long time:
that you know there are things your parents don't know.
Or maybe don't want to know. You can't always tell.

Like what Gus does in the living room that's only for company.
Always careful to take his shoes off.
Dancing around in his socks to keep the light gray carpet clean.
Those nights that Gus dances half naked
you say you're tired long before you are. Hope he'll stop
and put his pants back on.
He finally does. Says thank you for watching.
Claps his hands. Jumps up and down a few times.
Goes back out to the bungalow.

THE VILLAIN

This is a different trip to Elmer in the old green pickup.
Your father has a gun.
You and your brother are in the back of the pickup
where you like to ride with the wind in your hair.
Your mother didn't want you both to go.
Didn't want him to go either.
Don't worry, he told her. *I just have to teach Shattuck
that he can't push around the Jewish farmers anymore.*

Shattuck sells feed to the chicken farmers.
He also owns the Elmer Bank.
When egg prices dropped and the farmers didn't have enough money
to feed their chickens, Shattuck told them they didn't have to pay.
Then all of a sudden, he said they did.
Now he's taking away their farms.
Foreclosing is what your father calls it like it's a curse word.
It's what happened to Uncle Maier's farm. It's why
he had to take Tanta Rootie and the boys and go live in Brooklyn.
That made your father even madder at Shattuck
who you picture as the black-caped, evil villain who in the cartoons
comes for the daughter.

Your father, because of so much worrying about not having
enough money for chicken feed and for *putting food on the table,*
started selling Frank's Beverages. Seltzer and soda.
He leaves the house while the rest of you are still asleep.
Drives to Philadelphia to get the truck then sleeps in it
until just before sunrise when he starts delivering.
One day he brought home a blue glass seltzer bottle with
a fancy silver pump and his initials AT on the front.
The second floor of the farm's part barn, part garage

is where he puts crates full of blue glass seltzer bottles.
Cans of Frank's Soda. Orange vanilla crème, grape, cherry.
You wish he would sell soda forever. But he doesn't want to.

When selling seltzer and soda didn't bring enough money,
he started leaving in the afternoon to sell Tilo Roofing and Siding
door to door in Trenton every night. After knocking on as many doors
as he can, he sleeps for a while in the Frank's Beverages truck.
Not even long enough to dream, he part laughs, part complains.

In Elmer now, your father tells you and your brother
to stay in the back of the pickup while he
goes into the bank. He tucks the gun inside his jacket.
So Shattuck won't see it. Says he'll take it out
only if he has to—to show Shattuck he means business.
Don't worry, I won't shoot it are the last words he says
before he walks toward the bank steps. He doesn't say
what to do if Shattuck kills him.
If he never comes back to the truck.
Or if he kills Shattuck and the police come to take him to jail.

Soon as your father is too far to hear you or to think
you're scared, you tell Marty to get down low. Just in case
Shattuck comes out of the brick bank to shoot both of you.
You wait a long time.
Almost sure something really bad is happening in the bank.

Your father comes back. Doesn't say anything.
Just gets into the front of the green pickup
and starts driving. Fast.
You hope he didn't shoot Shattuck.
You wonder if he taught Shattuck a lesson
about leaving the Jewish chicken farmers alone.
About not taking away their farms anymore.

Will Shattuck stop giving the farmers the feed they need?
And if he does stop will the chickens all die?

What you do know is that you're glad
your father isn't dead. Glad he came back
to the green pickup with you and Marty in the back
and is driving it home now.

Even though your father is angry at the Hasidim
for not resisting Hitler, for talking more about faith than fighting,
for letting the Jews of Poland go to slaughter like sheep, still
he decides to send you, Marty, and Shelly to the *yeshiva,*
the Hebrew Day School opened by Chabad Hasidim
in Vineland. In a long building that reminds you of a chicken coop
but with classrooms inside.

The yeshiva has only one bus.
Your family lives the farthest away, so you get picked up first.
At seven o'clock in the morning. And dropped off last. At five o'clock.
A lot of days you leave and come back in the dark.
You don't mind. You would even come home later. Because
learning was never this delicious.

This school matches you. Feels like where you belong.
Where you want to be learning things.
Especially with Rabbi Mitnick.
Hebrew Studies every morning.
Secular Studies after lunch.
First thing you do every day is pray *Shacharis,* the morning service.
You all face east. Stand for most of it.
Some of it you pray out loud together. Some, silent. Though silent
is actually filled with murmurs, whispering the words to God
who is leaning close to hear them.
The boys aren't forbidden yet from hearing the girls' voices because
none of the girls, except for Gussie, are women yet.

Your favorite part is studying Torah with Rabbi Mitnick.
How he takes one word in a sentence and finds its three-letter root.

Because *Every word has a root.*
He searches for all the words he can find with the same root.
Like he's on a treasure hunt and everyone in the class is on one with him.
So excited by what he finds, he jumps up on his desk, lifts his arms high,
even cries sometimes because he's so happy to find
all the words and all the meanings *one root* can lead to.
How putting the same word in different sentences in the Torah
changes what the Torah tells us—what God wants to tell us
with that very word right there in that very place!
Feeling thrilled right along with Rabbi Mitnick,
your eyes fill with tears of happiness too.

With Rabbi Mitnick you learn the word *ecstasy.*
That going deep into words can make you feel it.

A girl named Michelle laughs almost every time that Rabbi Mitnick
lifts his arms. She makes the other girls laugh too
at the big circles of wetness under his arms.
At his sweaty wet shirt sticking to his chest and back. *So what?*
you want to turn around and tell Michelle.
So what? Who cares? Stop laughing at him.

Rabbi Mitnick does sweat a lot, it's true.
But you don't want him to be any different than he is.
Don't want him to change. To not get excited
about finding secret meanings hidden in the Torah,
always looking for clues that will lead him and his students
to new meanings.

Michelle is stupid. Even though that's not nice
to think about a person. You don't know why
she even comes to yeshiva if all she cares about is

stuffing her training bra with tissues
that stick out between the buttons of her blouse.

One day Rabbi Mitnick comes to your farm.
He plays ping-pong with your father on the new green table
in the cellar where the egg grader is.
Rabbi Mitnick gets even sweatier than usual. Takes off his tie.
Wipes his dripping face with the rolled-up sleeve of his white shirt.

After the game, he explains *the main reason* for his visit.
He thinks he solved the riddle of why you
get all the answers wrong on the arithmetic tests.
He says he checked closer. Turns to you, smiling.
Channahla, you actually got the right answers.
But to different problems.
Then Rabbi Mitnick explains to your parents
that you probably can't see what's on the blackboard.
You might need glasses.

When you finally get your glasses, you see the same problems
as everyone else does, even from the back of the room.
Rabbi Mitnick winks at you when he hands back your arithmetic test.
A *100%* in red on top.

Being at yeshiva is never even one tiny drop boring.
Even if Michelle says it is because she isn't
hungry for all the things Rabbi Mitnick wants to teach.
She just pays attention to his *sweaty armpits*.
You never laugh at the big circles like wet moons
under your Rabbi's arms. Raised like he is thanking God
for so many wonderful words.

At recess Gussie warns all of you,
a circle of sixth grade girls stooping behind bushes,
that the blood will come when
you are writing on the blackboard, so much
it will run down your legs,
stain the back of your skirt, and if it's a favorite skirt
the blood will ruin it
forever. And of course the boys
will laugh like crazy,
probably hold their noses,
because the blood kind of
smells funny.

Gussie knows things.

She got hers first in fourth grade when she was only nine.
Because her mother died, someone said. That's why it came early
and made her *chitchis* huge for just a nine-year-old girl.
Almost big as grapefruits.

None of you ask Gussie about her mother.
Or about how come she knows so much about blood and
that a girl will make a baby if she sits on a boy's lap. Or why
Gussie is the only one who needs a bra to hold her *chitchis* up
while the rest of you are so
flat.

I.

Your mother calls her *modern for a rebbetzin,* a rabbi's wife.
You call her fun.

Rebbetzin Blum wears a pixie haircut wig and bright red lipstick.
Her hair looks real. But it isn't, of course. The rule is that Hasidic wives
can't show their real hair except to their husbands.
With a wig, she doesn't have to wear a scarf. Her wig-hair is the color
of the inside of a grapefruit, the juicy red-orange kind not the pale yellow.
Rebbetzin Blum is short like a pixie too.

It's really hard to believe Rebbetzin Blum is married to
sourpuss Rabbi Blum who teaches Talmud to the boys across the hall
while his wife teaches the seventh grade girls who are not allowed
to study Talmud like boys can. Girls too old to pray with the boys
now that a few of you have started to *menstruate.*

One morning, Rebbetzin Blum decides to do something against the rules.
We are going to create a musical, she announces,
twinkling like a real pixie must, like any minute she might
pull a magic wand out of her desk drawer.
*It will be a musical about Purim. A musical means
you will sing everything. In Hebrew.* She winks. *Some people
might not approve. But that won't stop us.*
Then she whispers as if about to tell a secret she doesn't want anyone
except all of you to hear. *There are only two women in the Purim story.*
You already know that's Queen Vashti who got kicked out of the palace,
and Esther who becomes the Queen of Persia. Even though she's Jewish.
That means most of you will play the roles of men, Rebbetzin Blum says
like she might float up to the ceiling with joy—maybe because girls
will pretend to be boys. Maybe about her whole new idea.

After that, when Shacharis, the morning prayers, are all done,
the whole class practices for the rest of the day.
Rebbetzin Blum, like a conductor.

When Rabbi Blum knocks hard on the door to say
Your voices can be heard, Rebbetzin Blum puts her finger to her lips,
eyes shining. No one makes a sound. He stops knocking.
You hear his footsteps in the hallway, the door to his classroom close.
Okay, back to work! Rebbetzin Blum calls out, the finger
pressed to her lips a moment ago now waved like it's her magic wand.

One day she announces who will be who. You get picked to be
Mordechai, Queen Esther's uncle and advisor. You'll have a moustache
and a beard, wear your father's pants, shirt, jacket,
a black hat belonging to Rabbi Blum who finally gave up on
stopping the musical, but probably still covers his ears and
warns his students to do it too whenever your singing gets loud.
And it does. Louder and louder. Rebbetzin Blum tells the class,
afraid that Rabbi Blum's angry knocking will come again,
You must never apologize for raising your beautiful voices.

Nobody can believe it when Rebbetzin Blum rents a hall.
So the musical can be shared with *an audience. Much better,*
she says with a big smile, *than a musical happening in a room
for only the ones in that room and in that musical.*
Gussie tells everyone that she heard Rabbi Blum is *not going to attend
because God forbid should he be a part of such a shanda.*
Such a terrible disgrace.

If you were married to Rebbetzin Blum with
her orangish pixie hair, her big, red-lipped smile,
her beautiful voice and how, desks moved out of the way,

she dances around the room, you would feel
proud, not ashamed to be her husband.

II.

So many people have come, there aren't enough chairs.
A whole bunch of audience people stand in the back,
more against the side walls. Your father, who gave his chair
to an old woman, stands in a way back corner of the big room.

It's almost the part where you will have to step forward
to the front of the wooden stage. Alone.
A crowd of mourners behind you.
A solo, it's called.
You will pray for your people to be saved.
You have to be brave like the real Mordechai was. Even
if it means you might get killed. Just like Esther
could be put to death for her bravery.
The other barefoot Jewish men like you—Malka, Tova, Gussie,
Janet, Freda, Michelle—are wearing burlap bags
your father brought from the farm, empty feed bags with holes
he cut in the top for your heads to slip through,
holes on the sides for your arms. The burlap sacks are supposed to be
the *sackcloth* Mordechai and the other Jews put on with
ashes smeared on their faces. Ashes on your faces now
to mourn the decree that the kingdom's Jews be hanged.
The feed bags smell like a chicken coop. They're scratchy
and uncomfortable which seems just right for mourning.

Rebbetzin Blum signals that it's time. Time for Mordechai to step forth.
To lift his yearning prayer to God on behalf of all the Jews.

You walk slow like you practiced.
When you practiced though, your knees didn't feel

like they would fold up any minute. You take a deep breath.

Remember. *You are Mordechai.*

You take slow steps to the very front of the stage.

Look up to the heavens.

You start to sing. Slow as you can like Rebbetzin Blum taught.

As if each syllable is reaching all the way to God.

E-li

E-li

La-ma

A-zav-ta-ni.

You close your eyes. Think the prayer in English.

My God

My God

Why

have you forsaken me?

Forsaken means God is not with you.

No wonder Mordechai and the Jews are scared.

You get ready to sing it again.

Imagine the Jews in Persia soon to be hung.

Rebbetzin Blum didn't say to picture them. You just can't help it.

You think of how afraid they must be.

Think of your parents and what happened to their parents.

You picture people you don't know from places all over the world.

A lot of them are hungry. Cold. Barefoot.

So poor they don't have homes.

Tears start to roll down into your mouth. Salty tears

mixing with the ashes.

You squeeze your eyes shut. Sing straight up to God.

The words louder now.

Eli

Eli

La-ma
A-zav-ta-ni.

You feel the prayer go right through the roof. Then there is no roof.
Just open sky. Going up into it the syllables of your prayer.
You keep singing for all the people suffering in the whole wide world.
Beg God with your whole self to help them. *Please.*
Every part of you is begging
until all that's left
are the words *Eli Eli Eli.*

When you open your eyes, it feels like you are
coming back from somewhere else.
You don't know how long you were gone.
You are shaking inside your burlap sackcloth,
a trembling that won't stop.

You look out. See all the people in front of you
who you forgot were here, kind of like you forgot your own self
and even Rebbetzin Blum down in front of the stage,
tears making her eyes shine.

The day you find the pink smear on your panties,
it's a surprise.
Another surprise when a river of blood
doesn't gush out like Gussie said it would.
Even so you're glad to be home, your belly
hurting in a different and terrible way
that makes you bend over, arms around it.

When you call to your mother from the bathroom,
she comes. Closes the door behind her. Her kinder self.
You show her your panties. Try not to cry
from the hurt inside you and from how
gentle her touch on your cheek, her whispering.
My ketsella, this means you can have children.
A blessing from the Reboina Shel Olam.
You have not seen her this happy almost ever.
I call it my red friend, she says so quietly
your brother will not hear if he is by the door.
She comes every month. Now you have a red friend too.
Don't be afraid, ketsella.

She calls to your father. Tells him
not to come in. He should
go right away to buy more Kotex. We need them for someone.
She smiles at you. *Danken Gott, Thank God,* you hear him say
before it's quiet again.

There are no stores anywhere near your house.
You wonder where he will go
to find the blue box with the white K. *Sanitary Napkins.* That don't
look like napkins.
You wonder why he isn't embarrassed to ask in a store

for something so private. Just for mothers
and girls.

You've seen your mother put on her sanitary napkin,
how she pulls its front and back through hooks that
hang down from a kind of garter belt, the whole contraption
to keep the napkin from sliding around in her panties.
Gussie says everyone can tell when you're bleeding
not just by all the blood, but because sanitary napkins
make your panties bulge.
For now, you bunch up toilet paper,
press it against your peshy in case the blood
pours out like Gussie warns it will.

Your mother says you can stay in the bathroom.
Outside the door she tells your brother and sister
Leave Ehni alone. They should knock only if one of them *has to go*
You will just step out while they do. Can come back and
be alone right after.

Finally you hear the car
and next thing your father is at the bathroom door.
Bubalah, he says, voice soft. *I have something for you.*
You wish he would just leave the blue box outside the door
but don't say so. Instead you open the door just a crack.
Stick out your arm.
I brought you these, he says. You hear
the tears in his voice.

You open the door all the way.
Mazel tov, my tochter, my dear daughter, he says,
both arms stretched out to you.
In one hand a brown paper bag hiding the box.
In the other he's holding roses.
A whole bouquet of them. Red like blood.

You can hear *Itsy Bitsy Teenie Weenie Yellow Polka Dot Bikini* blasting from
the jukebox in the snack shack at A Lion's Beach.
Three songs for a quarter. Sometimes they play *Itsy Bitsy* three times
in a row. A stupid song that sticks in your head because they play it a lot.
Some girls at A Lion's Beach wear bikinis. You don't, of course.
Tan Shoes and Pink Shoelaces plays. Another song you sing along with
but think is stupid. *Come Softly to Me* is one of your favorites.
But they never play *Come Softly* on the jukebox. Now it's *16 Candles.*

One of your favorite things is to dance. But *never ever* in the snack shack at
A Lion's Beach where the teenagers dance. You dance with a cement post
in the cellar when Dick Clark and American Bandstand
come on the radio. After you finish packing the eggs at the grader and
no one is left down in the cellar anymore, you jitterbug with the post,
so good for pushing against. You even do slow dances with it.
Marty saw you once from the cellar steps and started yelling.
Annie's kissing the post. Annie's kissing the post.
Another time you wanted to kill him. Well not really kill him.
Just make him shut up and mind his own business.

Now your father comes to where you're sitting on the sand,
wrapped cozy in a towel, drying off from swimming. Not like
the teenagers who never go in the water because they're afraid
their bikinis might slide off.

Your father says he needs a pack of cigarettes, *right now.*
He wants you to go get them. You don't want to. Don't say yes.
Don't say no. He's just doing this because he doesn't want you to be shy,
which you are and even more shy about going where the teenagers are.

To get to the wooden door with its top half open where people buy things, a person has to go into the small wood building with the jukebox and the teenagers in it. Your eyes water and get blurry just walking up the sand hill toward it. They sell Fudgsicles and Creamsicles at that half open door, but you would sooner not have any than have to go in there to buy one. Your father knows this even though you never told him. He holds out a quarter for a pack of Kents. An extra quarter to play three songs in the jukebox.

He says you have no choice. You have to go because he's telling you to. He pulls you up. When you're standing, he opens your hand. Puts the quarters into it. *Now go.*
You don't.
I said go. What? Are you afraid they'll eat you? When you don't move, he hollers, *I don't understand you. Nobody is going to bite your head off.* He pushes your back. *Go!*

You take small steps. Drag your feet in the sand. You aren't afraid anybody is going to bite your head off. You just aren't like him. You never will be a person who's not afraid of anything. You aren't like him and never will be. No matter how hard he pushes your back. Or pushes you with his words. He can't force you to be different than you are.

The music gets louder the closer you get. Your eyes get blurrier. You'll never be one of those *confident* teenagers who talks loud and mixes with a big crowd. You just aren't a crowd person. And you don't want to be. Well, maybe sometimes, just a tiny bit. Once in a while you do wish you were confident like he is. Like the girls in the snack shack who talk loud and laugh and wear bikinis and are not one single bit shy or embarrassed, whose eyes never get blurry when they have to look at lots of kids at once. They never think for a minute of running away and hiding. Never wish to be a turtle and not come out when they don't want to.

Getting closer you look down. That's how you will go in and buy his
cigarettes—looking down. You'll only look up for a second when you
have to give the money and take the pack from the person
behind the half open door. You hear that stupid song again.
Two three four, tell the people what she wore. It was an itsy bitsy
teenie weenie yellow polka dot bikini that she wore for the first time today.
You wish you would never hear that song again. But even more you wish
you had the power to make yourself invisible. To disappear into thin air.
You think of the name of a song you heard once. *Smoke Gets in Your Eyes.*
You don't know the words but think that song is about what you feel now.
If you could be surrounded by smoke, that would be the next best thing
to being invisible.

You have an idea when you are about to go up the three wood steps.
You'll *pretend* to be invisible. Pretend that no one can see you.
Only you will know you are there. For just one magic minute,
the person selling Kent cigarettes will hear your voice, see the quarter
in your hand, trade the pack for the quarter and then won't see you.
Of course, you won't put the other quarter in the jukebox. Though
it would be funny if *Come Softly to Me* all of sudden started to play
and nobody knew how it happened.

I see you kneel then stretch out your lean girl's body
to find the miracle. Smooth-skinned. Silent. Hidden.
A ballooning watermelon
beneath a curling leaf umbrella.

You had no idea where that fruit,
whose seeds you use for spitting wars at the beach,
came from or that it could grow on this farm
where the mean chickens in their coops
peck at you when you dare approach their warm eggs.
But this life, this born thing
would do no harm
resting here, heavy. Bold. Growing.

The bigger miracle is that your father made this happen.
That he with thoughts of loss and livelihood hanging over him
every waking moment and even in his dreams
would take the time to plant a watermelon seed.
And even more surprising, tend
a green fruit swelling like a pregnant belly.
Pregnant with itself. With sweetness and juice.

How glad it makes you,
pressing your ear to the ground each day,
lifting the leaf cover to see
this fruit growing soundlessly, almost shyly.
To watch it grow your father's patience into
almost something to touch.

One hot Saturday afternoon, he carries the heavy orb to the picnic table.
A king bringing treasure to his people.
He cuts it with his sword-knife. Serves up the luscious, red bounty.

He does not plant a seed again, does not kneel to
watch the ripening, to smile at your delight,
to say, even gently some days,
It's not ready yet, ketsella.
You have to be patient.
For some things, you just have to wait.

Lucky is buried here on the ranch. Under a mound near
the rusty tractor whose seat you'll stand on like usual
to conduct the invisible circus. *Ladies and Gentleman,*
Come One, Come All, you'll announce, making the trees laugh.

But first you go to Lucky's grave, stretch yourself over it,
press cheek and ear to hear Lucky breathe. You tell Lucky
in your mind to hers how much you miss her. That you are
so so sorry those drunk people hit her with their swerving car.
And that the dog doctor couldn't fix her hurt leg.

Lucky already knows
that you wish your father hadn't taken her in the green pickup
all the way to Camden and left her there so he wouldn't have to
shoot her. You tell her again like you did
when she came limping back that you know how much
she must have loved your family to limp all the way back
on her infected leg, which got much worse,
until your father had to borrow a gun
to take her out of her misery.

Lucky knows that was the saddest day in your life,
the minute you heard those gunshots coming from the ranch.
Two of them.
Your father wouldn't let you watch.
I hope what he said is true, you whisper to Lucky now,
that it didn't hurt.
Because he got the bullet right between her eyes on the first try.

You don't tell Lucky that your mother hit you when
you couldn't stop crying after the gunshots. That she

wouldn't stop screaming *Just a dog!* That you should only cry like that
for people. Murdered. Too many to count, treated worse than dogs.
Not even buried. *A hynt nish a mensch! A dog, not a person!*
Do you hear me? A dog! You can't cry like this for a dog!

You don't tell Lucky even now, how your mother tried to
pull off the black sweater you got from her drawer, and put on
because you don't have any black clothes. How you fought to keep it on.
Then refused to put your shoes back on when she tried to force you.
Because another way to mourn is wearing socks without shoes.

Crying now on Lucky's grave, you don't tell her
how much you wanted to mourn for her the right way.

You first ask Marty when he is hanging upside on the swing set.
If he remembers. The white porch you used to rock on together
when you were old. *I remember,* he says, quick getting right side up.
The one with two rocking chairs. We had white hair.

You picture the big open front porch wrapped in sunlight,
you and Marty smiling at each other, eyes twinkling.
We were so happy, you say. Marty who usually doesn't agree
with anything nods. Smiles like he is seeing it now.
We laughed a lot on that porch, he says.

You ask your mother on a long ride to Sears Roebuck
to buy bags for the vacuum cleaner and underwear for your daddy,
Where is that porch Marty and me used to rock on when we were old?
She wrinkles her face like she doesn't understand your question.
Remember? Marty calls out, leaning forward from the back seat.
The one with the two big rocking chairs? Where were you and daddy?

Your mother says she has to pay attention to the road and
please stop bothering her with pretend games when she is driving.
This isn't a pretend game. But she can't tell.

You ask a few times after that day. Wonder if maybe
she is pretending not to remember
because she doesn't want you to find that porch.

A child's imagination! she says one morning when you ask.
Stop talking such narishkeit. It's foolishness. You are children.
You were not old. You will become old, but knock on wood—
and she does—*not for one hundred and twenty years.*

You whisper Marty's name from your bed that night. He's awake.
Remember when we were old and we rocked next to each other?
Yeah, Annie, I remember, he answers. Both of you quiet after that.

You don't ever ask your mother again. But more than once in a while
you close your eyes and see you and Marty rocking together,
laughing and laughing, sunshine in your long white hair.

Jack sits at the head of the table in the mustard-colored
fake-wood bucket seat that swivels. But Jack is not swiveling.
He's tilting back in the bucket in a way the rest of you aren't allowed to.
Like any minute he might put his feet up.
Pipe to his lips, he grows the smoke cloud around him.
Your mother turns at the sink, wipes her hands on her apron.
Ehni, she says, *loves to read.*

You wonder why she's telling Jack this. Like she thinks it's good.
Something to be proud of. Or at least to act proud of in front of Jack.
Their only American friend. The only friend who talks without an accent.
Who went to college. A lawyer. They *admire* Jack more than anyone.
He admires them too. For their bravery. For surviving.
How your parents and Jack are together reminds you of that song,
We Belong to a Mutual Admiration Society.

Jack, did you know that Ehni loves to write too?

You wish your mother wasn't telling Jack this. She never told *you*
that reading and writing are good things to do. The opposite.
She usually says it's selfish to love them as much as you do.
To want to do them more than other things. Maybe she's telling him
because you know how to read English and spell English words right.
Like an American.

Jack puffs on his pipe. Looks at you through his smoke fog and smiles
like he isn't sure whether to believe your mother or not. He tilts back
even more in his bucket. Stares at you over the top of his glasses,
raises his eyebrows. The way he moves his neck back and forth
reminds you of a chicken. *Really?* he asks. *You like to write, Anne?*

Something about the way he asks, not just because he keeps the e silent,
makes you want to run out of the room. But that would be rude.
So you stay, standing still at the opposite end of the table.
You watch Jack look like he might tip backwards out of his chair
which you don't dare to secretly wish might happen.
Really? he repeats. *Let's find out more about this, shall we?*

Your wanting to be invisible is getting stronger by the minute.
But you know that's impossible, except in cartoons.

Tell me then, Anne.
He says your name like he's trying to teach your mother
the correct American way to say it.
Which authors have you read?

You know what the right answers would be.
After all, your favorite card game is *Authors*.
You could say, should say: James Fenimore Cooper.
Henry Wadsworth Longfellow. Nathaniel Hawthorne. Sir Walter Scott.
But you would be lying.
So, you say *Nancy Drew. Oh—and Agatha Christie.*

You only just began reading Agatha Christie books a week ago.
But you don't tell Jack. Or that sometimes you read
two Agatha Christie books in one day.
You also don't tell him that if you could, you would rather read
than do almost anything else.

Even before Jack laughs then starts coughing—smoke floating
from his mouth and nose like he was a chimney,
you already know Nancy Drew and Agatha Christie don't count
as real authors.
Maybe now Jack will forget about you. Will turn back to
talking to your parents about the stock market and Zionism.

Children should be seen not heard is how it usually is when
once in a blue moon anyone comes to visit the farm.
Not being seen or heard is fine with you when it's Jack.
Even if he did come all the way from Brooklyn.
Jack is your parents' hero. Not yours.

In his own private cloud,
reclined like some kind of king on a throne in a kitchen that isn't even his,
Jack keeps looking at you.
You know, he says, *you can fool them, but you can't fool me.*

I wasn't trying to fool my parents or you, you want to yell. But don't.
Your parents will of course agree with Jack not you.
Better to keep your angriness at Jack inside. If only you could disappear.
You hope he'll get bored talking to a stupid little girl
who reads Nancy Drew.

Your parents say you like to write. Is that true? he says.
You barely nod.
He's touching something you don't want him to touch.
You don't want him to come near and touch it at all.
Well, is that true?
Looking down at the table you say a quiet
yes.

I want to tell you something for your own sake, Anne.

You don't want your name in his mouth.
Would rather stay *Ehni* than hear this man take your name.

For your sake, Anne, he says louder now, sitting forward
in his bucket chair. *Don't get your hopes up.*
People who aren't native English speakers don't ever
become fine writers in that language.

This is something you never thought of before.
Of course. It makes so much sense. You should have known this.
But you didn't until *right now.*
You will *never* be a great writer. *Never.*
Tears rise into your eyes from the ocean of sadness inside you.
Even though he's right, you don't want to let one single tear
spill out in front of Jack.

Your secret wish is crumbling. To be such a good writer
that you would be in the *Authors* deck.
A card with your name on it. Four cards.
All the books you wrote in a list.
The only woman there now is Louisa May Alcott.
You wanted to be the second one.
But you were dreaming. *A fool.*
Just like your father and mother say about you.

The *biggest foolishness,* they always say, is you believing
people are really good inside—that there are
more kind people than mean ones.
You wanted to write one day about the kindness in people.
To write about what's beautiful and about what's sad in the world.
So people could feel better. So they wouldn't feel so alone.
You wanted to help people pay attention to crickets. To rain.
Wind. Dew. Sky. And to children, to the feelings of children.
You wanted to help people be kind. Most of all to help people be kind.

You were going to write about the light of goodness
that is in everyone. Even though sometimes it's hard to find
and you have to really try and how you have to be especially still
to notice it in mean people.

So many things you wanted to tell about in writing.

But being the daughter of refugees
is not something you can change.
You should have known you could never be an author in the deck.
It feels like Jack just shot you with an invisible bullet.
Like he killed something in you for good
even though you didn't fall down. Even though you keep being polite
to your parents' best friend. An American. A lawyer.
Who went to college. Who talks with no accent.
Who must know the truth.

You saw her for the first time inside the television.
Wanted right away to go to her. To walk with her.
To hold her hand if she would let you. And if she
didn't want to hold hands, you would say *Okay, Ruby*
and walk behind her so that nothing would hit her not even the names
shouted by what the TV man calls
an angry mob.
You know that names hurt even if they don't break bones.
Some people throw stones at the little girl who has
rolled-down white ankle socks like yours
and is going to a school where people don't want her
like they didn't want you in Jacksonville.

Until right now you never saw a girl who knows what it's like.
When just being who you are and different from other people
makes them hate you. And there's nothing you can do to change it.
When hiding doesn't work because they already saw you
and besides where would you go?

Ruby. That's what the TV announcer says is her name.
Ruby Bridges. You want more than anything for Ruby to know
she is not all alone. You are with her.
You can't make the angry mob go away but you could
walk with Ruby so she wouldn't have to walk alone.
The tall men with suits, who don't smile, walk with her.
But that's different from having a friend, another girl,
who loves you just the way you are.

In bed that night you whisper to Ruby under your pillow.
Tell her you are close even though you're far away.
Tell her you wish you could crawl into the television set, go to her.

But you can't, so you stay with Ruby in your mind
where no one can separate you from her.
You ask God if your dreams can mix with Ruby's
so you can be together at night when Ruby doesn't have to
walk through the shouting mob up those steps
that remind you of the steps to Jacksonville School,
where if a genie had come to give you one wish,
it would have been to be invisible.
You wonder if Ruby ever wants to be invisible too.
There are so many things you want to ask Ruby.

In the morning, you start writing letters to Ruby Bridges.
You write that you know, too, how it feels to be *the only one*.
Ask if she ever gets bellyaches in the morning, if
her eyes get all blurry when she stares straight ahead.
You promise to keep her secrets safe.
You want to keep *her* safe too. But how?
You don't have a gun like the guards probably do and besides
you're just a girl like her. *Ruby*, you write, *if I could,
I would chase away the people who call you names.*
You fall asleep holding Ruby's hand.

Ruby's kindness shows through every time you see her.
She never yells things back at the angry people
with their signs, their shouts, and their meanness,
who don't even know Ruby.
You close your eyes, imagine harder
how to get to Ruby through the TV.
The whole time your parents think you are quietly watching,
you don't tell them that in your mind you are
crawling into the television box and by magic getting to Ruby,
so happy to see you because she knows, like you know,
that you are more than sisters. You are the same.
The only thing different is that Ruby has darker skin than you.

Ruby can't hide her skin. The color of her skin is what the angry people hate the most. They act as if darker skin is a contagious thing so they have to keep people with dark skin away not to get cooties. Cooties is what the kids at Jacksonville School didn't want to catch from you.

One night you hear Ruby in her bed. She is whispering a message that goes into the night sky over both your heads. *Sometimes I feel lonely and scared—but also brave. I am happy you are my friend.*

In the morning after seeing more mob people around brave Ruby, you tell Ruby in your mind that you don't *really* know what it's like to have dark skin. You wish you did know so you could understand *exactly* how she feels. You've been thinking, you tell her, that a person could maybe keep it a secret they are Jewish. If they don't talk with an accent. Don't carry a lunchbox with strange, not-normal food in it and don't do other things that help people figure out they're Jewish. But Ruby can't keep her skin color a secret. You're sad about things being easier for you than for Ruby. It's not fair.

You ask Ruby if she's angry at you for sometimes being glad that you weren't born with dark skin. Does she still want to be your friend? Can you still be best friends?

That night in her bed, Ruby says *Yes, of course.* Because she knows you believe brown skin like hers and beige skin like you have are both okay. You both know one kind isn't better than the other kind.

You are still best friends and will always be, she whispers,
no matter if other people might try to keep you apart and don't know
you belong together. One girl in two different bodies
in two places in America.

SUBURB

I see you seeing the street you're going to live on.
Number 1110. Half of a house. A *duplex*, it's called.
A half house in a long row of houses all exactly the same,
except for some of their checkered garage doors
painted different colors, with matching front doors.

House after house after house. Too many to count.
Lined up along a wavy sidewalk. So close together
you think of matches crowded into a matchbook.
Pretty soon, you'll be like one of those matches.
It won't matter if you want to be or not. Your parents already decided.
And you can't stay living on the farm alone without them.

Your mother is allergic to everything about the farm.
The straw in the coops. Feathers. Dust. She's even allergic
to dogs, one reason Lucky wasn't allowed into the house.
You know she won't miss the farm. Won't miss the pale blue sky
or the dark almost black one. The quiet that never ends.
If a person can be allergic to quiet, your mother is.
The quiet that's on the farm won't be around a duplex in *a suburb*.

You didn't know what a *suburb* was. Now you do.
A place where all you can see are rows and rows
of same exact duplexes. The only thing different besides
the color of their doors is the numbers on them.
Even on one side of the curvy street. *Odd* on the other.
No mailboxes. Just a shiny flap low on the front door
for letters to slide through. The other thing
that makes a suburb a suburb is a shopping center not too far from it
and a bus that stops in the suburb to take you there.

You know right away the worst part of living at 1110 Gregg Street
is going to be no trees. No trees in the back or the front.
Just crewcut grass. Nowhere to hide.
Nowhere to sit and write in your diary.
No place to be all by yourself, which you want as much
as your brother wants food and your father schnapps at night.
What your parents think is important is not what
you think is important. Like trees near your house.
Because how can a person live somewhere without trees?
you wonder in the back seat, hiding your tears
on the way home to the farm from the boring suburb.

When you get closer to the farm, your mother, mixed in
with complaining, announces how happy she will be when
the farm is not the home she has to come back to anymore.
You cover your ears when she starts saying again all the things
she hates about the farm. Most of them, things you love.
How lonely it is. How far the farm is from everything.
Dead quiet and lonely. She repeats *lonely* a lot.

Maybe if she knew how friendly and alive the willow is.
How the tall blue-green grass on the ranch sizzles.
How the sky at night winks and smiles with its stars.
How the wind loves caressing faces, if you let it.
But it's not like that for her. It doesn't matter to her
that the farm doesn't have a number
and there isn't a single other house like it on Iona Road.

You have no choice but to go with them.
At least Kathy will come and your diary.
But where will you go with them to be alone?

You cry yourself to sleep again. So much that
your pillow gets wet from your wishing to be free
and that children got to decide things.

❧ DESTINY

You and Herman Strauss get picked to be
Valedictorian and *Salutatorian* at graduation from yeshiva.
You never heard either word, and for sure neither did your parents.

You have to write essays. Yours will be in English.
Herman is writing his in Hebrew. You never wrote
an essay before, decide to call it: *Israel, Land of the Bible.*

You write the story of being a grain of sand
who witnesses the Holy Land since ancient times.
Being blown around from place to place lets you see things
in the Sinai desert, in Jerusalem, on a mountain
in the Galilee, at the bottom of the Dead Sea.

The day of graduation you go first. You stand up,
put your six pages on something called a *podium*,
in front of rows and rows of folding chairs behind the yeshiva.
Before starting to read you look out and greet everyone.
Right then the wind lifts your pages off the podium.
Quick you chase and finally catch each one. Count to make sure
you got all six, put them in order, take page 1 from the pile,
set it straight in front of you. Just before you start reading,
you decide you better put one elbow down on the other pages
so the teasing wind won't steal your essay again,
which makes you stand kind of crooked while you read.

When you finish, Rabbi Blum stands and reaches
something to you, careful not to touch his fingers to yours.
A gift for being Valedictorian. It reminds you of your diary.
But it's not a diary. It is the smallest prayerbook you ever saw.
With a zipper that wraps all the way around it. You want to unzip it

but don't yet. Instead you
say thank you to Rabbi Blum, pick up your pages,
wave goodbye to the audience, and sit down
in your folding chair in the front row. It's Herman's turn now.

Pretending to listen to Herman, you quietly unzip the little book,
feel its onionskin pages, peel apart some sticking to each other.
You look down at the see-through pages, covered with crowded
Hebrew letters way too tiny to read. You look at Herman
without really listening. You think about this being
your last day in yeshiva. After you move to that suburb,
you'll have to ride a bus to Woodrow Wilson Junior High School.
A public school. It feels like you're going back to jail.

You look down at the crinkled pages of your essay
that tells the story of a little grain of sand, tossed and blown
by wind, but also by her curiosity, her wanting to learn things.
You would rather be a grain of sand that stays on the farm.
You zip the small prayerbook closed. Rest it in your lap
on top of the pages that almost got away.
All of a sudden you think about how you are like
a page being torn from a book you belong in,
a page about to be blown far away with
no one to bring it back.

You ask if you can stop packing things and
just for a few minutes go outside
to say goodbye to the farm.
Your mother nods.

The sun makes the diamonds glisten in the driveway sand.
You slide your feet like a skater, leaving smooth trails
on your way to the swing that you're too big now
to take to heaven. You run your hands along its rusty leg.
Say thank you.

Across the driveway you climb the rickety steps
to the loft over the old part-garage, part-barn filled once upon a time
with Frank's beverages and bees that ganged up on your father
every time he tried to move them out.
If you had a cherry soda now, you'd turn over
that one wood crate left here upside down. No matter the cobwebs.
You'd sit down on it. Open the soda, careful because it's warm
not to let it spill over. Sip it. Slow. Hope no bees will come around.

You climb back down.
Head for the chicken hospital, long empty of sick chickens.
It squats on stacks of cinderblocks, door ajar like an open mouth.
Two small windows, its eyes. You wink back.
Did it always tilt like that? you wonder from under
the needly skirt of your favorite of the three tall pines.
You think of the crinoline bought for going to birthday parties,
stiff and flared like this pine that sheltered you and your diary
more times than you will ever be able to count.

You go to the clothesline next.
Fewer angels gather now in a chorus line to greet you.

Maybe because there aren't any wet sheets for them to smell,
to wrap themselves with, to play hide and seek in with you.
They don't lift their legs as high now when they dance.
You wonder if they are sad. If they will
keep playing on the clothesline
without you to watch.
You whisper that you will *never ever, long as you live,*
forget them.

On the ranch, you stretch across Lucky's mound. Smaller now,
like it's sinking. You wonder about Lucky's body, what
you'd see if you undug the place she got buried.
But you would never do that. The mound over her seems
a good place for her to be resting in.
Your tears wet the dirt.

You stand. Squint into the sunlight. See rainbows in your tears.
Still as you can be, you listen to the silence on the ranch.
Silence is your favorite thing to listen to. The listening changes you.
Makes you more like silence.
You close your eyes.

Start to spin. Slow at first.

Arms stretched out right and left so that everything on the farm
is in your embrace, you turn and turn and turn. Every blade of grass.
The ants crawling over and under the bridges grass makes for them.
Every diamond in the sand.
The arching willow branches. The willow's wild dance.
The empty coops, their smells that still linger
long after the last chickens have been sold off.
The softness and songs of baby chicks.
The memory of lilacs.
You bring the sky into yourself. Its colors, moods.

When Hurricane Hazel peeled the roof off chicken coop number 4.
When snow stopped the world.

Spinning, you remember.
Taste of a ripe, juicy watermelon.
Fruit plucked with fear from a scribble of blueberry bushes,
feeling sorry for the man on the other side of the tangle.
String bean tree hanging over the deepest best puddles.
Cool cellar with its abandoned egg grader and
your dancing partner, the tall dark handsome post.
Bungalow emptied of Gus who begged to stay—
but who your father drove to Camden, ordering him
not to come back the way Lucky did or he would shoot Gus too.
Your father didn't mean it. Said it was the only way Gus would listen.
You picture coal carried into the bungalow, a few round chunks
falling into the crystalline snow like black stars
you were too late to catch.

You keep spinning. The trees spinning around you
as if holding hands.
You thank them for being here. For being trees.
Wish you could take them with you for shelter and love
on barren Gregg Street. Last night you hugged your willow so tight,
you were one. Her roots, your roots.
Her stillness, your stillness.

You spin faster. Don't let the dizzy topple you.
Until you are not making yourself spin but being spun.
A spinning happening on the inside too,
what you love drawn deeper and deeper into you.
Everything on the outside, now inside.

When you leave
you will bring the farm with you.
In you.

You fall back onto the spinning plate of earth,
arms and legs spread like when you make a snow angel.
You open your eyes. See the spinning sky. Know
you will always be able to find your way
home.

AFTERWORD

Hello again, Dear Reader,

I wanted to greet you on the other end of your passage through this book.

An earlier version of *BLOUSE,* ended with a Part II, these words:

And the five-year-old become woman?

I can forgive my mother,
her rage meant for the ones who left her
without choices.

I pick up the blouse,
the pink lace. Lift the child to my lap and
holding that small hand in mine,
guide her to stitch together
what was torn apart.

I didn't know when I wrote those words that helping the child gather the torn pieces and stitch them together would describe the process of writing *Angels on the Clothesline.*

Initially, almost all the vignettes in the memoir opened with *I see you.* As I wrote into the scenes, I chose to be present to the joyous *and* the painful moments in my childhood. I cannot change what happened or what did not happen. But witnessing with compassion changes me from the inside out. I also emerge from writing this memoir with greater perspective and a more seasoned compassion for my parents.

After leaving the farm, I encountered many more twists and turns in my life, some very difficult. A knowing, with me since childhood, sustained me even through the darkest of times. I never forgot what I saw in Terry, in Lucky, and in the stars, or the ecstatic freedom of spinning, swinging, riding into the wind, and writing to an unseen companion, a source of love I trusted was listening. Over time, I came to know that source as always present within me.

I used to think that if given the chance to rewrite the script of my life, I would do so in a heartbeat. Not anymore. As it turned out, my experiences, instead of shutting me down, opened and formed my heart. And not only that. My experiences seeded a passionate commitment to cherish, honor, and protect children, which has inspired my life's work.

For over five decades, I've worked as an educator, a chunk of that time with children and parents in under-resourced communities. I spent time in South America with children so deprived of basic human rights and dignity that they and their families had to scrounge in the city dump for materials with which to shelter and clothe themselves, competing with the vultures for food scraps.

As a young mother, I studied child development and special education, then co-founded a multicultural, bilingual preschool and day care center named A Kangaroo's Pouch/*El Buche del Canguro* where all the languages, nationalities, skin colors, food, and holidays of community members were respected and valued. We housed the school in a former synagogue that we raised funds to renovate in a city with a tragically high rate of child abuse.

When I was pregnant with my second child, I moved to a rural area and soon began hosting writing circles for children, often out-of-doors with my daughter in a backpack carrier. The groups evolved into safe and inspirational havens for teen girls and now women to find and free their voices.

My work as a writing mentor has continued for almost forty years. During the pandemic and sheltering in place, *"I see you ..."* became a particularly potent writing spark, a portal into greater self-awareness and self-compassion for members of my online writing groups.

Had I not faced the challenges in my childhood, I likely would not have felt called in the ways that I have. My life experiences also led me to find paths to healing and to inner freedom. Meditation has been a huge blessing in my journey; EMDR (Eye Movement Desensitization and Reprocessing therapy), an invaluable healing modality. Al-Anon Twelve Steps Family Groups awakened me to the effects of codependence and supported me in making healthier choices. The unconditional embrace of nature and the ever-refreshing process of writing continue to be essential on my life's path.

In the wake of World War II, no one was addressing the post-traumatic stress disorder from which both my parents suffered. Thankfully, there are now new frontiers in the understanding of intergenerational trauma, the intersections of personal and collective trauma, and of trauma and spirituality. We are also becoming more enlightened about post-traumatic strength and resilience.

This is my story, but aspects of it belong to children and adults all over the world who have been shamed, feared, or punished for being different, for being *other*. Immigrants and their children. Black Americans and others who have been racially targeted. Those demeaned because of their ethnicity. Individuals shunned for their sexual preference or gender identity. Persons who have been devalued or shamed themselves because of size, or physical or intellectual disabilities.

To be clear: this book is as much for readers who don't have direct experience of the above, but who live in a world with others who do.

Angels on the Clothesline is a story of vulnerability and resilience. My story also reveals the sensitivity, innate creativity, and wisdom of children. It would be my dream come true were this memoir to awaken deeper understanding and respect for children, along with broader protection and advocacy on their behalf.

I also hope that *Angels on the Clothesline* invites you to *see* yourself, including your inner child, with open-hearted curiosity and compassion. When we bring loving awareness to the fear and pain *within us*, we become more able to truly heal the divisions *among us*.

Deep listening, to our own selves and to each other, is key to healing. Sharing our stories can build bridges over what may seem irreconcilable chasms between us. As Valarie Kaur writes in her wonderful book,

See No Stranger: A Memoir and Manifesto of Revolutionary Love, "Deep listening is an act of surrender. We risk being changed by what we hear."

I wish I could see *you* now, dear reader, sit down with you, maybe on a park bench with a breeze delighting us, to listen to some of your stories and to talk about your experience of reading this book.

Since we can't rendezvous that way right now, I warmly welcome you to please come visit my website, www.anituzman.com, and write to me via my contact page. *I would love that!* You have my promise that I will do my best to reply.

With awe for our tender and invincible humanity,
Ani

I SEE YOU:
An Invitation to Write into Compassion

NOTE: *If you have experienced extreme, untreated trauma, then the following might best be done in a safe container with a therapist or another skilled guide.*

As well as sharing my story of seeing and being seen, *Angels on the Clothesline* is an invitation into *your* seeing.

Writing or typing *I see you* at the top of a blank page, although appearing to be a deceptively simple act, can lead into deep and wondrous inner territory.

Try it. Write *I see you.* Then let come what comes. As you write, allow yourself to follow where the writing leads. Let the writing take whatever form it chooses, be it stream of consciousness, a letter, a poem, or bits of all of these. The one that is being seen might be you—at any age, in any circumstance. Or you might *see* someone close to you. Or a stranger.

Just be present. See with compassion. Notice if you confuse compassion with pity. Pity limits, makes excuses, blames. Compassion frees.

Compassionate witnessing frees the love held captive in unhealed trauma, in self-judgment, in blame of oneself or others, in regret. Self-compassion brings the balm of love to our wounds, accepts how we or others may have shut down, and wraps us in patient kindness.

With our compassionate presence, we can touch the experiences in our *now* that need acceptance and loving. It never is too late to heal what we regard as the past. Because in truth there is just one continuous, flowing now. And it is always the right time to see with love.

Try it. *I see you ...*

NOTE: *Extensive research proves the profound, long-term benefits to our physical and mental health of writing about our emotions and our traumatic experiences.*

For more inspiration related to the healing joys of writing,
please visit www.anituzman.com.

A NOTE TO PARENTS, EDUCATORS, AND OTHERS WHO TEND AND LOVE CHILDREN

First of all, thank you for doing such vitally important work and for your caring.

I hope that one of your experiences after reading *Angels on the Clothesline* is to feel inspired to tend to your *inner* child with curiosity and an open attentive heart. To bring presence and awareness to our own tender places—not just our wounds but also our passions and longings—allows us to be more present to the needs and experiences of those in our care.

To invite onto our laps and embrace *all* the parts of ourselves, particularly those we have disowned perhaps in fear or shame, is to meet them with love. In doing this inner work, we become more available to truly *see* the children and others in our lives. Rather than seeing through the veil of our own unfinished business, we become able to greet others with clearer perception that allows us to sense their inner light and to be aware of their essential goodness. To see and be seen in this manner frees the seer and the seen.

Every one of us who takes responsibility with self-compassion not self-blame, who doesn't blame the past or blame others, brings a gift to the children and youth in our lives and to the world.

Writing is one way to engage in this process of knowing and freeing ourselves. *I see you* is both a sit-down writing practice and an orientation to life. Using *I see you* can be a portal into self-awareness and into a deeper connection with the *other, the stranger.*

Part of *I see you* is *I hear you.* I warmly invite you to call forth and listen to the stories of the children and youth in your life. Encourage them to tell their stories, perhaps first to themselves through writing or drawing pictures. If more suited to a particular child, their *telling* could be through dance, song, or other art forms. Help to create safe spaces—*be a safe space*—where they can share their experiences, truths, pain, passions, and joys.

A great thing to remember in all this, which you probably already know well, is that our children are our teachers as much as we are theirs. They shine light on the places in us that need that light.

Our children are also our dance partners as we learn to listen to the silences, the spaces between the words as well as the words, and to move with more grace and joy. On this dance floor, we also get to practice forgiveness of ourselves and our partners for the inevitable awkwardness, for spacing out, stepping on each other's toes, or any of the other ways we might seem to mess up. Thankfully, the music of our love and our commitment calls us back to the dance floor.

So, thank you again for all you do and for who you are. Thank you for recognizing the vulnerability of our children and their right to profound respect and wise protection. Thank you for all the ways you value and nurture children's sensitivity, wonder, creativity, and irrepressible spirits. Thank you for tending to those qualities within you.

With immeasurable gratitude,
Ani

I will be offering online and in-person Writing Circles for children, youth, and adults inspired by the theme, "I see you ..." and by other themes in my memoir. I will also be developing writing resources that invite self-compassion and compassion for others. Please visit my website www.anituzman.com for more information. I welcome hearing from you about your particular interests.

Acknowledgments

For the loving and skilled support of the following souls, my deep and abiding gratitude.

Melissa Tefft, thank you for who you are and for how you reflect me back to me, so that despite all my filters I get to *see*.

Susan Olshuff, thank you for loving not only the children I have borne, but the books as well.

Meg Fisher, thank you for your deep listening as I read every vignette in this book to you over the phone during the pandemic. Thank you, too, for how you see the wonder in children—and for never feeling sorry for young Annie.

Editor Peg Moran, my endless gratitude for how you have held this book *and* young Annie. Thank you for the countless emails sent in the middle of the night (night owl that you are), waiting to greet me in the morning with reassurance that this was a book to stick with. And for that particular note describing a reader someday hugging *Angels on the Clothesline* like little Annie hugged the books she loved—what can I say?

Nancy Richler, you helped feed my inner fire at the beginning when shame might have quelled the spark that led to this book.

Rosie Pearson, your reaction to the darkness in my story helped me to find even more light.

Laura Duffy and Karen Minster, for your design skills and the joy of partnering with you to birth another book, thank you, thank you. Editor Deb Nichols, your keen eye and editorial prowess are gifts.

And finally, to my daughter Nomi and her amazing tribe, thank you for the rain of your love.

About the Author

Ani is an award-winning poet, an author, and a writing mentor. Her historical novel, *The Tremble of Love: A Novel of the Baal Shem Tov* has been hailed as "a rare gem of transformative fiction."

After many years as an early childhood educator in the Boston area, including co-founding A Kangaroo's Pouch, *El Buche del Canguro* Day Care Center, Ani started a new phase of her life. Ani moved from the city to the country, gave birth to her second child, and began offering writing groups for children in the woods. In the early 1980s, Ani created the Amherst Writers and Artists (AWA) Youth Division, then went on to found and direct the Dance of the Letters Writing Center where, for more than forty years, she has inspired people ages eight to eighty-eight to find and free their voices.

With more books of her own to birth, Ani also wants to help liberate the stories in adults and children throughout the world. A particular dream is to bring together diverse groups, including those who have considered each other enemies, using writing to turn within and toward each other.

Ani lives in New England where she savors meditating, the changing seasons, her changing grandchildren, and the countless ways there are to share love.

For more about Ani and her work, events, and to stay in touch, please visit https://anituzman.com.

You are warmly invited to join Ani's Inner Circle. (Free)

You can also follow Ani on Facebook, Instagram, and LinkedIn

Ani loves to hear from readers!

Thank You

Thank you for reading *Angels on the Clothesline*.

If you enjoyed this book, please let others know about it via word of mouth, social media, or asking your library or local bookstore to stock it.

Also, *please* consider posting a review online at sites where books are sold. Your rating and review, even just a few sincere words, could help a reader connect with a book they might love.

Thank you in advance for sharing the word and helping *Angels on the Clothesline* reach other hearts.

Made in United States
Orlando, FL
15 March 2024

44818351R00150